Sweet inspirations

by
Pam Manning

Table of contents

Kansas City Star Books

Sweet Inspirations

Author: Pam Manning
Editor: Judy Pearlstein
Design: Cheryl Johnson, S&Co. Design, Inc.
Photography: Aaron Leimkuhler
Technical Editor: Jane Miller

Copyright © 2007 The Kansas City Star Co.

Published by Kansas City Star Books.
First Edition
ISBN 978-1-933466-32-3
Library of Congress Control Number: 2007923827

Printed in the United States of America
Walsworth Publishing Co., Marceline, Mo.

To order copies, call StarInfo at (816) 234-4636 and say
'BOOKS.'

or order online at www.PickleDish.com

I have always loved sewing and creating things. I was born in the Adirondack mountains of New York state and grew up in a family of eight children. I learned to sew at my grandma's knee and, soon thereafter, she taught me to use her treadle sewing machine. She often saved quilt patterns out of the Sunday paper to make us quilts. Our family moved to Bedford, Indiana, a small midwestern town, in 1988 for my husband's job at GM. I enjoy volunteer work at church, playing with my three grandsons, gourd painting and taking trips on our Harley.

Acknowledgments

I would like to thank Lorraine Hofmann for introducing me to Folkart/Primitive quilting and the http://groups.yahoo.com/group/PrimFolkApplique2/.

I want to thank Warren Kimble, one of America's greatest Folk artists, for allowing me to include my rendition of his famous "Round Barn" in the quilt. I have loved your work forever!

And thank you, Doug Weaver, for giving me such wonderfully talented people to work with: Judy Pearlstein, Cheryl Johnson, Aaron Leimkuhler and Jane Miller. I have learned so much from you.

Dedication

I want to dedicate "Sweet Inspirations" to my mother-in-law, Ellen Manning, who found her love for quilting late in life. Her life was truly a sweet inspiration of giving and doing for others. I will always miss her.

And to Don, my childhood sweetheart and husband of 37 years, your encouragement and love have meant everything to me.

And above all, to the Lord, who continues to teach me to live, love, laugh, learn and pray.

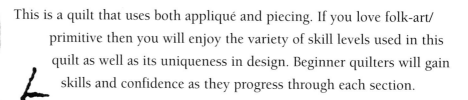

This is a quilt that uses both appliqué and piecing. If you love folk-art/ primitive then you will enjoy the variety of skill levels used in this quilt as well as its uniqueness in design. Beginner quilters will gain skills and confidence as they progress through each section.

Fabric Basics

Always use good quality, 100% cotton fabrics for quilting. They are more enjoyable to work with and wear better in the long run. They will shrink and fray less than synthetic blends and poor quality cottons.

Appliqué Technique

Trace all your appliqué pattern pieces onto the dull side of freezer paper. (Freezer paper pattern pieces can be used over and over again) Transfer any letters, placement markings and any grain lines at this time. A simple light box is great for this. Cut them out on the line. Lay the shiny side down on the right side of your fabric and press. Cut out 1/4" away from your pattern piece. Assemble all your appliqué pieces on the background fabric. (You can use your light box to help you get them in the correct position if need be.) Hold them in position with any acid-free, washable glue of your choice. When you are ready to appliqué, trace around your pattern piece with chalk or washout blue quilting marker and clip the concave (inside) curves. The bigger the curve, the more clips. Don't clip too far in, but close enough that it will turn under without a pucker. I like to remove the freezer paper at this point and needle-turn the seam under. Begin by threading a couple of needles with an 18" thread the same color as your appliqué piece (preferably cotton thread). Come up through the underside of your background fabric and out through the fold of your appliqué seam. Using the tip and shaft of your needle, turn in your seam allowance. Go into your background fabric, opposite your thread in the appliqué piece, coming up again 1/8" from your last stitch, a little under your seam fold and out through the fold, catching at least three threads. Repeat with your needle going back in again opposite where you came out. Keep your stitches 1/16"- 1/8" apart (more stitches on curves and points and a little wider on straight seams). Snug up your thread a little as you appliqué to have nice finished seams. (If it's puckering, it's too tight) If you are new to appliqué, take your time when you begin, and learn the technique right. By the time you finish the first quilt, you will be much more proficient and eager to start your next one. Do some blocks up ahead and put a little sewing pack next to the door. Then, when you need to go somewhere that you have to sit idle for awhile, you can grab your pack as you leave and keep yourself busy with appliqué.

Terms

scraps - 1/8 yard will be sufficient when the pattern calls for scraps.

binding - Usually cut on the bias but not necessarily. Join seams for binding using the diagonal seam method.

Big Stitch - creates a very nice look on primitive and folk art quilts and wall hangings. Mark your quilt with the disappearing ink or chalk of your choice, using the Baptist Fan with arcs spaced 1 1/2" apart. You can get the stencil from "The Stencil Co." It is product #SCO-173-07. Mark the first small arc and then skipping two, mark the next, etc. (You will have five rows in the arcs when you are done). Mark as many sets as you can get in your hoop. (I recommend an 15-18" hoop.) Start the next row the same as you started your first, with the arc stencil lined up on the edge of your fabric. Use #10 crochet cotton and a #5 crewel embroidery needle (or #24 Chenille needle will work. It needs a big eye and sharp point). The stitch is 1/4" on the front. Mine is 1/8" on the back. It can be 1/4" on the back. You can either bury your starting thread in an appliqué piece or on the edge of the quilt or let all of your knots be seen on the back of your quilt for a more primitive look. If you choose the primitive look, knot your thread leaving a 1/2" tail and let it stay on the back of the quilt, tying on a new thread (on the back), as needed, with a "surgeons knot" (right over left twice and left over right twice).

Sign and Date Your Work

Things you may wish to include:

- Who made this quilt and maybe a little about you or your life
- Original or pattern name
- Your city and state
- Who the quilt is for and their information
- Inspiration: things happening around you right now in your family or world

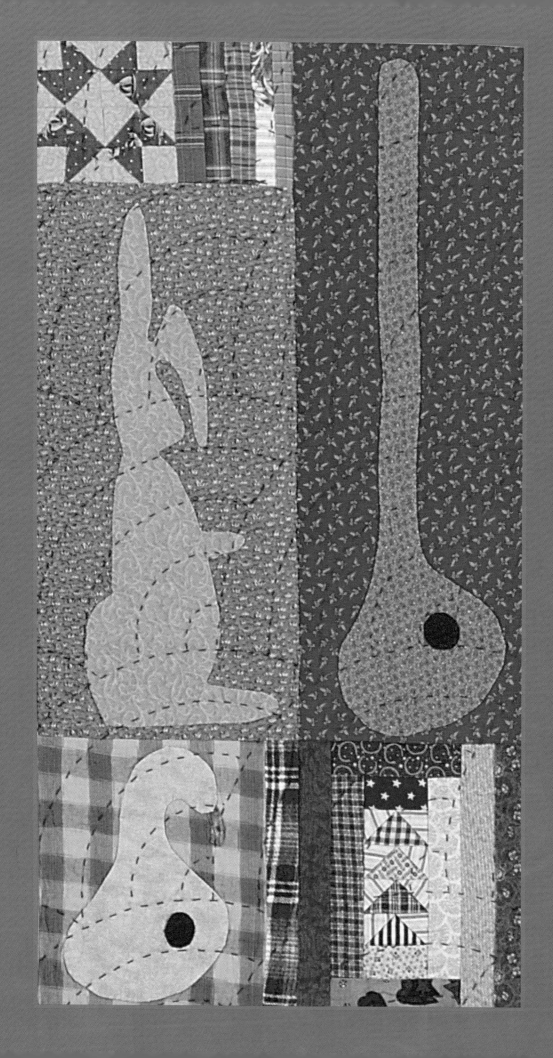

Add seam allowance on all appliqué pieces when cutting.

A: 8 POINT STAR
Finished size is 4 1/4" square.

Fabric Requirements
• Scraps of blue and tan

These instructions will give you enough for two 8-point stars, one for block A and one for block G in the Blue Section. Seam allowance is included, but either cut generous blocks or sew a scant 1/4" in your seam allowances.

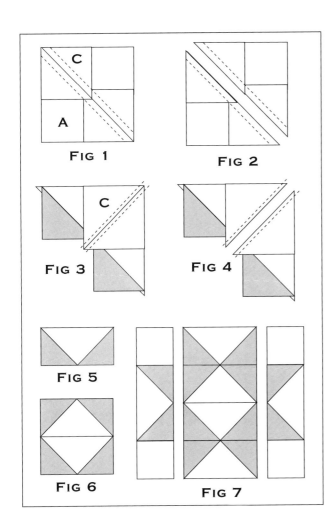

FIG 1

FIG 2

FIG 3

FIG 4

FIG 5

FIG 6

FIG 7

Block Construction
• A - Cut 3 tan 3 1/4" squares
• B - Cut 8 tan 1 1/2" squares
• C - Cut 12 blue 1 7/8" squares
• With a straight edge, draw diagonal lines on the wrong side of all (C) squares.
With right sides together, lay 2 of the blue (C) squares on the larger (A) square at opposite corners with the lines going from corner to opposite corner. (Fig. 1) Stitch a scant 1/4" on both sides of the drawn line.
• Cut apart on the drawn line. (Fig. 2) Press seams toward small squares (C).
• With right sides together, lay one of the marked C squares on the sewn unit and stitch a scant 1/4" on both sides of the drawn line. (Fig. 3)
• Cut apart on the drawn line. (Fig. 4)
• Repeat until you have 12 of these (flying geese) units. (Fig. 5)
• Join 2 units together as shown in figure 6 for the middle square. Press seams to one side. Join another flying geese unit to either end of the middle square as shown in fig. 7).
• Join a (B) tan square on each side of 2 more (flying geese) units. Press seams to the outside. Join to the center unit as shown to make an 8-pointed star block.
• Repeat for the second block.

B: 5 ROW RAIL FENCE

Finished size is 4 1/4" x 3 3/4".

Fabric Requirements
• Red and blue plaid scraps

Block Construction
• Cut 5 strips 1 1/4" x 4 3/4". (I cut strips a little longer and trim the finished block to the accurate size.)
• Sew together lengthways.
• Trim to 4 3/4" x 4 1/4".

C: BUNNY BLOCK
Finished size is 15 3/4" x 8".

Fabric Requirements
• One fat 8th green for the background
• Gold scrap for the bunny

Block Construction
• Cut background 17" x 9".
• Appliqué bunny to block.
• Trim to 16 1/4" x 8 1/2".

D: LONG HANDLE DIPPER GOURD
Finished size is 20" x 7".

Fabric Requirements
• One fat quarter red for background
• One fat 8th medium brown for gourd
• Scrap of black for hole
• Scrap of darker brown for stem

Block Construction
• Cut background 21" x 8".
• Appliqué the gourd to the background, the hole and the stem to the gourd following the picture on page 6 for placement.
• Trim to 20 1/2" x 7 1/2".

E: SMALL BIRDHOUSE GOURD
Finished size is 8" x 7".

Fabric Requirements
• One fat 8th brown/cream for background
• Gold and black scraps for the gourd

Block Construction
• Cut background 9" x 8".
• Appliqué the gourd and the hole to the background following the picture for placement.
• Trim to 8 1/2" x 7 1/2".

F: FLYING GEESE BLOCK
Finished size is 8" x 8".

Fabric Requirements
• I used scraps of blue/cream stripes and plaids, and light gold/brown stripes for the geese and various scraps of red, cream patterns, brown check, dark blue pattern and plaid.

Block Construction
For the center of the block, you will make 4 geese 2" x 1" finished. Make this block using foundation paper piecing OR:
• A - Cut 1—3 1/4" square.
• C - Cut 4—1 7/8" square.
• Make 4 flying geese as in block A on page 7.
• Cut 2 red and cream rectangles 1 1/2" x 2 1/2".
• Cut 2 cream and brown rectangles 1 1/2" x 6 1/2".
• Cut 2 cream and brown rectangles 1 1/2" x 4 1/2".
• Cut 4 rectangles (rust, cream, dark blue and plaid) 1 1/2" x 8 1/2".
• Sew the red 1 1/2" x 2 1/2" rectangle to the top of the geese unit, and the cream rectangle to the bottom.
• Sew the cream and the brown 1 1/2" x 6 1/2" rectangles to the left and the right side of geese unit.
• Sew the cream and the brown 1 1/2" x 4 1/2" rectangles to the top and the bottom.
• Sew the rust and the plaid 1 1/2" x 8 1/2" rectangles to the left side. Sew the cream and the dark blue 1 1/2" x 8 1/2" rectangles to the right side.
• Press. The block should measure 8 1/2" square.

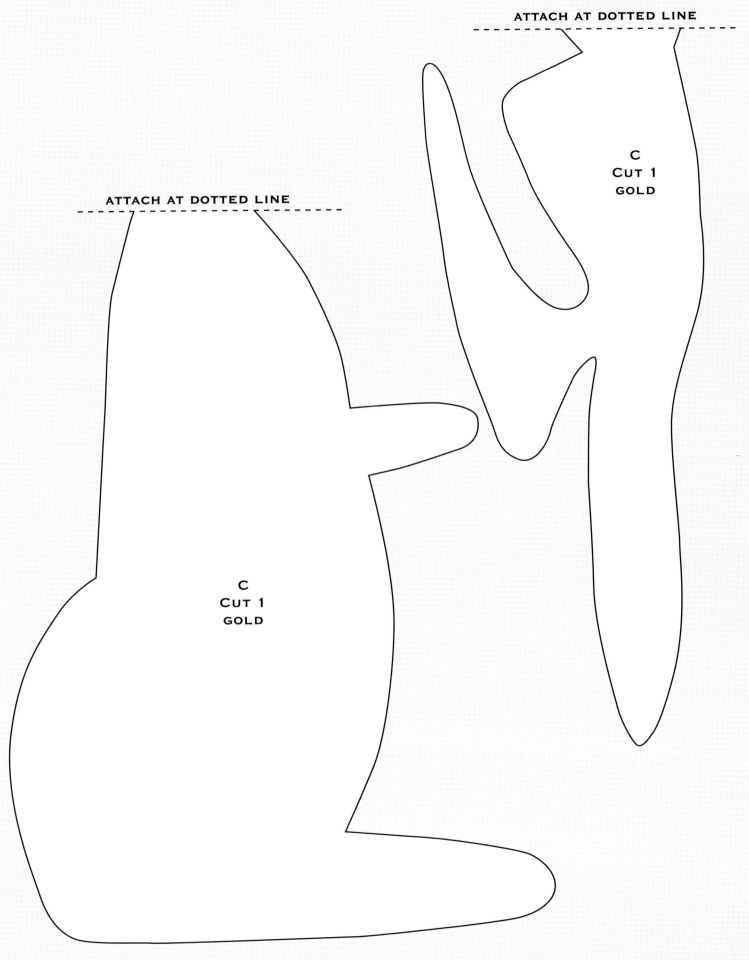

ATTACH AT DOTTED LINE

C
CUT 1
GOLD

ATTACH AT DOTTED LINE

C
CUT 1
GOLD

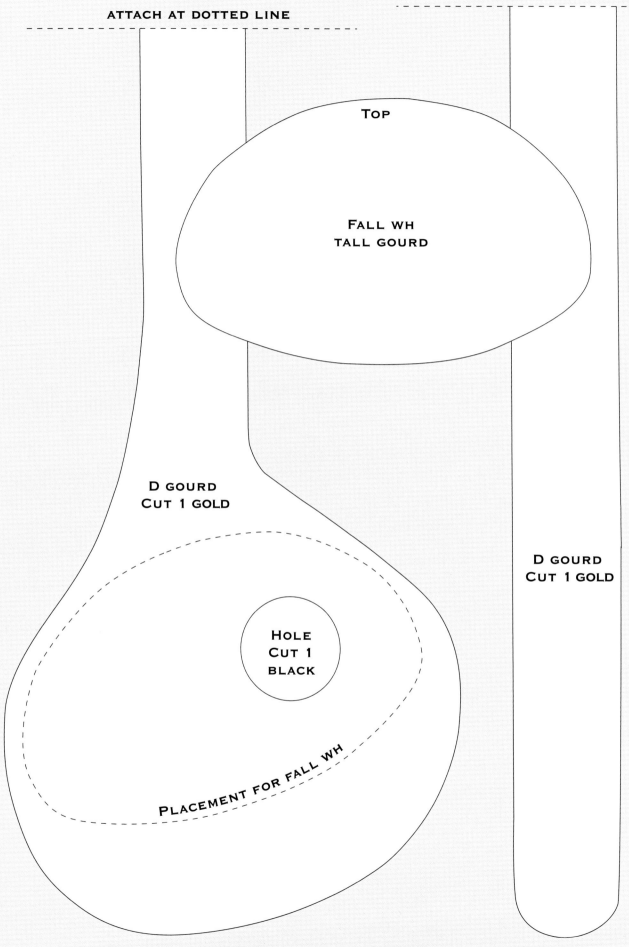

ATTACH AT DOTTED LINE

ATTACH AT DOTTED LINE

Top

Fall wh
tall gourd

D gourd
Cut 1 gold

D gourd
Cut 1 gold

Hole
Cut 1
black

Placement for fall wh

10

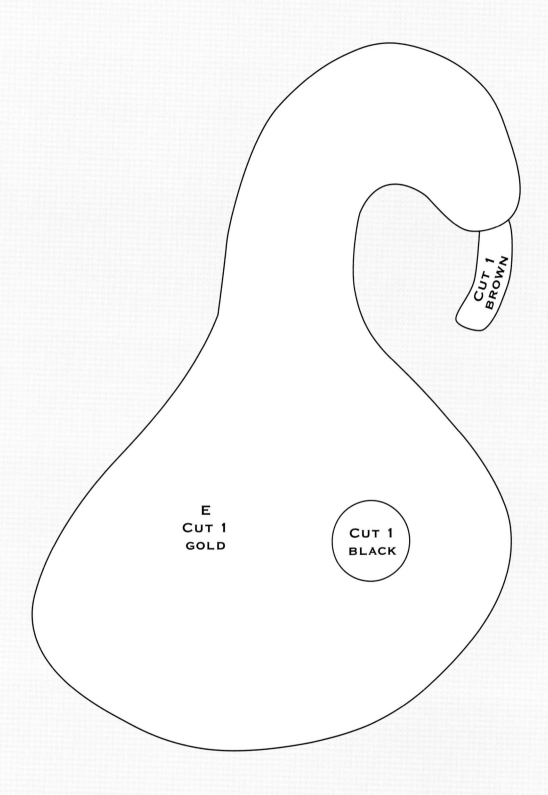

E
Cut 1
GOLD

Cut 1
BLACK

Cut 1
BROWN

G: THE 8-POINTED STAR
See block A in the Green Section

H: FIVE POINTED PIECED STAR
Finished size is 12 3/4" x 4 1/4".

Fabric Requirements
• Scraps of red/brown stripe and white pattern
• Scraps of white/black crackle pattern for background

Block Construction
• Use the paper piecing technique for this block. Use freezer paper templates for this block. They are easy and accurate and can be reused. Copy the pattern provided onto the paper side of freezer paper, transferring your letters and grain lines with each piece. Cut out your templates and iron the shiny side of the freezer paper to the right side of the fabric, leaving enough room for a 1/4" seam allowance. Cut a 1/4" seam around each piece. Sew together using your freezer paper as a guide for your seam line.
• To assemble, join A to B to C, D to E to F, H to I to G, ABC to G, GH to DEF.

I: EGG BASKET
Finished size is 10" x 12 3/4".

Fabric Requirements
• One fat 8th red/brown for background
• Scraps of orange/gold basket weave pattern for basket
• Co-coordinating stripe for basket trim
• Creams, whites and tan for eggs

Block Construction
• Cut background 11" x 14".
• Cut piece 1 and 10 from your basket fabric. Appliqué in place. Leave space open to insert the ends of 11 and the diamond shape 13A-13B.
• Cut pattern pieces, except for pieces 11 and 12, from freezer paper. Iron the shiny side to the right side of your fabrics. Cut around adding a 1/4" seam allowance on all pieces.
• Cut eight eggs out of different whites and creams and appliqué in this order. Start with 3, 4, 5, 6, 7, 8, 9, with egg 2 last.
• Cut piece 11: 12" x 1 1/8" for the basket trim. Sew a basting stitch along the edge of the stripe and draw up until it fits along the top edge of the basket.
• Place 11 over the edge of 10 and the eggs, keeping it slightly curved, tucking the ends under pieces 1 and 10. Glue and appliqué in place.

Add seam allowance on all appliqué pieces when cutting.

• For pattern pieces 13A, 13B, 14A, 14B, 14C, and 14D, lay the outside edge of the pattern, on the edge of a stripe on your fabric and iron in place. Cut a 1/4" seam allowance around your pieces. Put these aside.
• For piece 12, the handle, cut a strip 6" x 1 1/8". Again, sew a basting stitch along the edge and draw it up to give it a slight curve. (Use diagram.)
• Appliqué 12 (handle), and 13A and 13B in place. Finish appliquéing the back of the basket.
• Sew 14A and 14B together. Sew 14C and 14D together. Sew 14AB to 14CD to make a diamond. Press. Appliqué in place over handle.
• Trim block to 10 1/2" x 13 1/4".

J: COW
Finished size is 12 3/4" x 7".

Fabric Requirements
• One fat 8th red and cream plaid for background
• Tan scrap for body
• Black scrap for spots
• 18" of 6-ply floss (match to body material)
• Small piece of Heat and Bond

Block Construction
• Cut background 14" x 8".
• I used Heat & Bond to attach the cow spots and then zigzag stitched the edges, or you can appliqué them in place.
• Braid the floss (tail should be about 5"), tie the end in a knot. Attach under the cow with a strand of 6-ply floss, leave hanging, knot 1 1/4" down, and trim at knot.
• Appliqué the cow body and legs with legs and tail tucked under the body.
• Sew ear pieces, right sides together, turn right side out and fold end seam to the inside. Stitch closed and attach ear to cow head at base, curving it like a real ear.

K: LETTERS BLOCK
Finished size is 17" x 12".

Fabric Requirement
• One fat quarter blue check for background
• Scraps of gold, reds, black, and white for letters

Block Construction
• Cut background 18" x 13".
• Appliqué letters in place.
• Trim to 17 1/2" x 12 1/2".

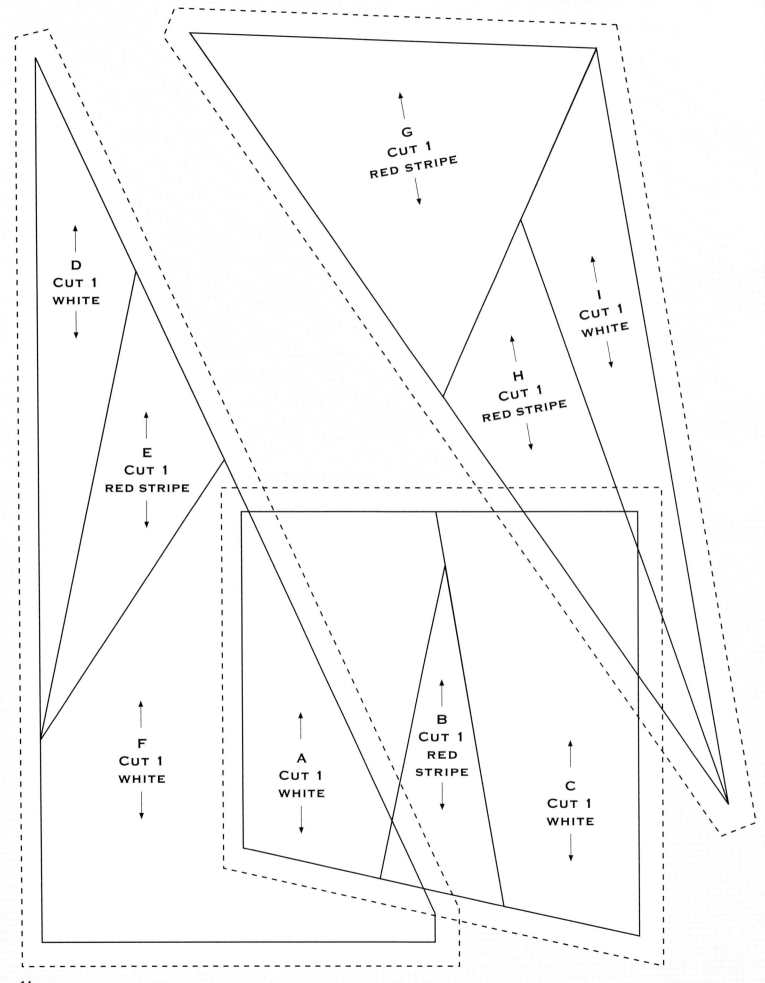

G
Cut 1
red stripe

D
Cut 1
white

I
Cut 1
white

E
Cut 1
red stripe

H
Cut 1
red stripe

B
Cut 1
red
stripe

F
Cut 1
white

A
Cut 1
white

C
Cut 1
white

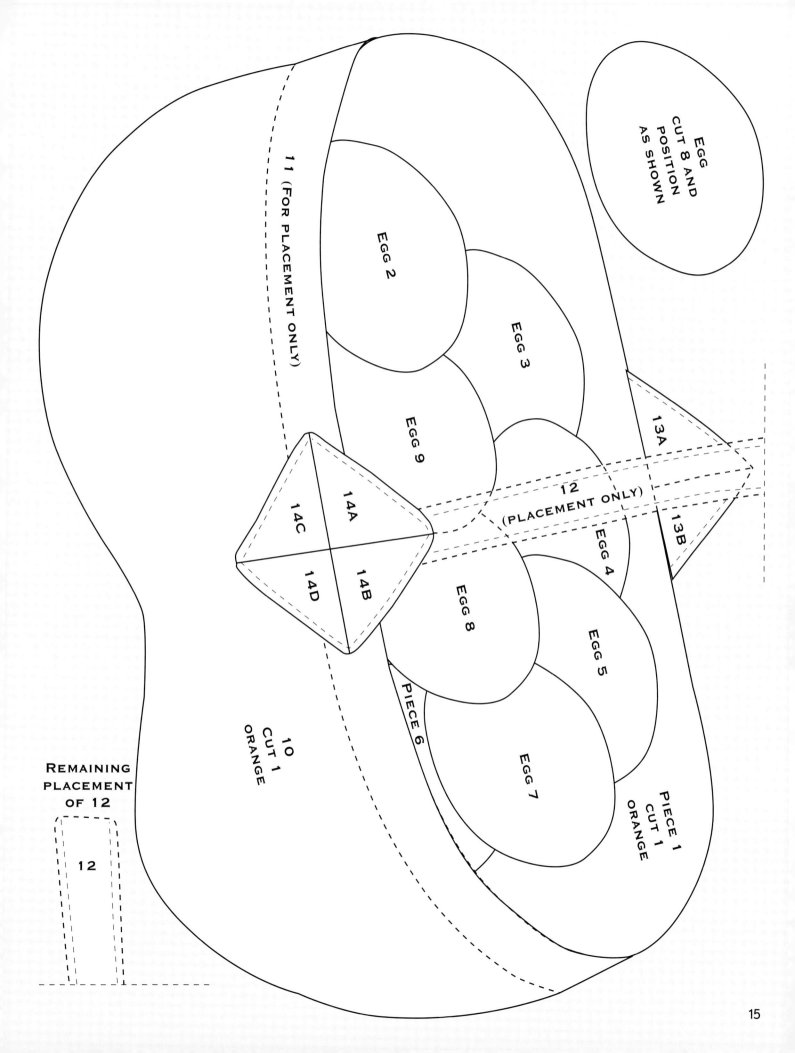

EGG
CUT 8 AND
POSITION
AS SHOWN

EGG 2

EGG 3

EGG 9

13A

11 (FOR PLACEMENT ONLY)

14C

14A

14D

14B

12
(PLACEMENT ONLY)

EGG 4

13B

EGG 8

EGG 5

PIECE 6

EGG 7

10
CUT 1
ORANGE

PIECE 1
CUT 1
ORANGE

REMAINING
PLACEMENT
OF 12

12

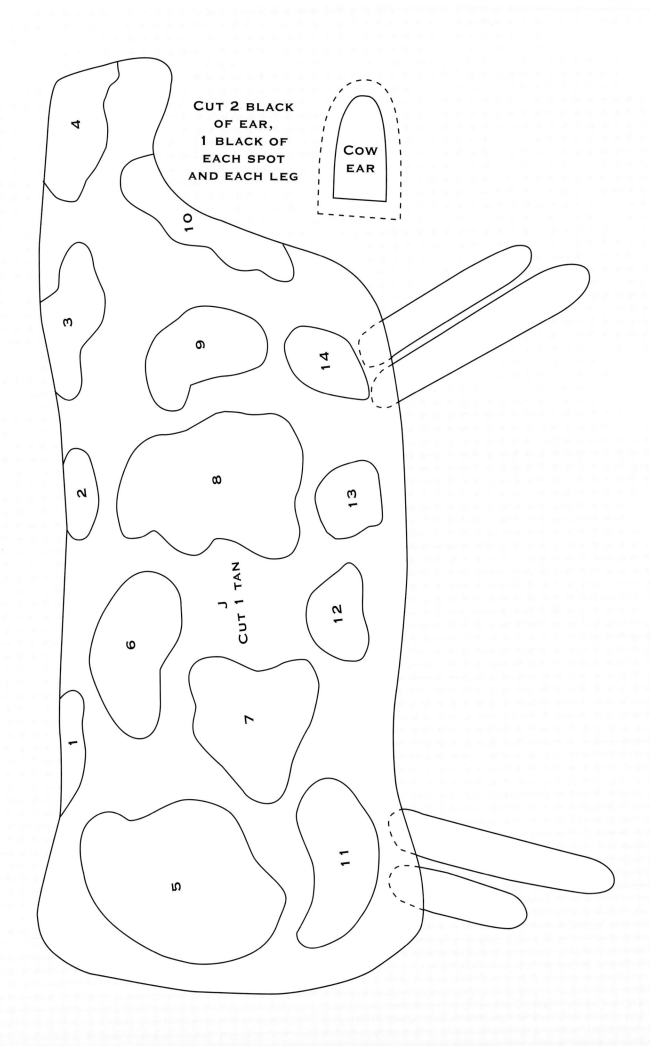

CUT 2 BLACK OF EAR, 1 BLACK OF EACH SPOT AND EACH LEG

COW EAR

4

10

3

9

14

2

8

13

J
CUT 1 TAN

6

12

1

7

5

11

FALL WH - L

QUILT - L

17

Add seam allowance on all appliqué pieces when cutting.

Zb: CAT BLOCK
Finished size is 11" x 5".

Fabric Requirements
- Green scraps for background
- Gold scraps for the cat
- Black and white scraps for stripes.
- Two 1/2" buttons for eyes
- 3 ply black floss

Block Construction
- Cut 12" x 6" for background.
- Appliqué stripes onto cat and cat onto background.
- With 3-ply black floss, make nose and whiskers, and attach 1/2" buttons for eyes.
- Trim to 11 1/2" x 5 1/2".

Aa: ROSE BLOCK
Finished size is 14" x 2".

Fabric Requirements
- Cream scraps of for background
- Green scraps for stems
- Red scrap for rosebud

Block Construction
- Cut background 15" x 3".
- Cut 13" x 1 1/4" green strip for the stem.
- Sew wrong sides together lengthways using a 1/4" seam.
- Trim seam to 1/8". Insert your 3/8" press bar and press with seam hidden in back.
- Appliqué rose, stem, and leaves to background as in photo.
- Trim to 14 1/2" x 2 1/2".

Za: ROUND RED BARN
Finished size is 14" x 22".

Fabric Requirements
- One fat quarter blue and cream for sky
- Scraps of two small green checks for grass
- One fat eighth or scraps of red for barn
- Cream scrap for stone
- Black scraps for roof, rooster
- Green and gold check for tree tops

- Bleached muslin for windows, door and pinnacle strips
- 1 1/2" x 1" flag cut from fabric or embroider your own (I cut.)
- Embroidery floss
- Light brown 6-ply floss for tree trunks
- Dark brown 6-ply floss for fence
- Black 6-ply floss for flag pole, birds

Block Construction
- Cut background 15" x 23".
- Appliqué from the bottom of the block up, starting with the grass. Add the trees.
- For the windows, use a Sharpie ultra fine point permanent marker. With a light touch applied in a couple of steps so the fabric doesn't get saturated and bleed outside the line, make the black windowpane. The line on the double doors may be made with a marker or embroidered.
- Stem-stitch the tree trunks, fence, flagpole and birds.
- Trim to 14 1/2" x 22 1/2".

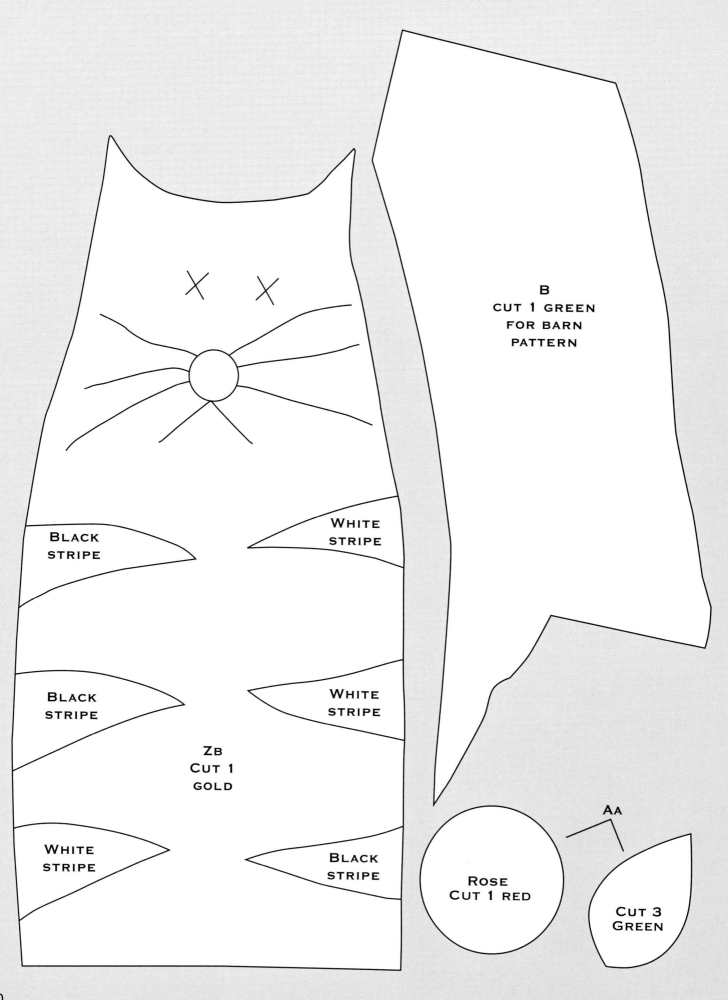

BLACK
STRIPE

WHITE
STRIPE

BLACK
STRIPE

WHITE
STRIPE

Zв
CUT 1
GOLD

WHITE
STRIPE

BLACK
STRIPE

B
CUT 1 GREEN
FOR BARN
PATTERN

ROSE
CUT 1 RED

Aa

CUT 3
GREEN

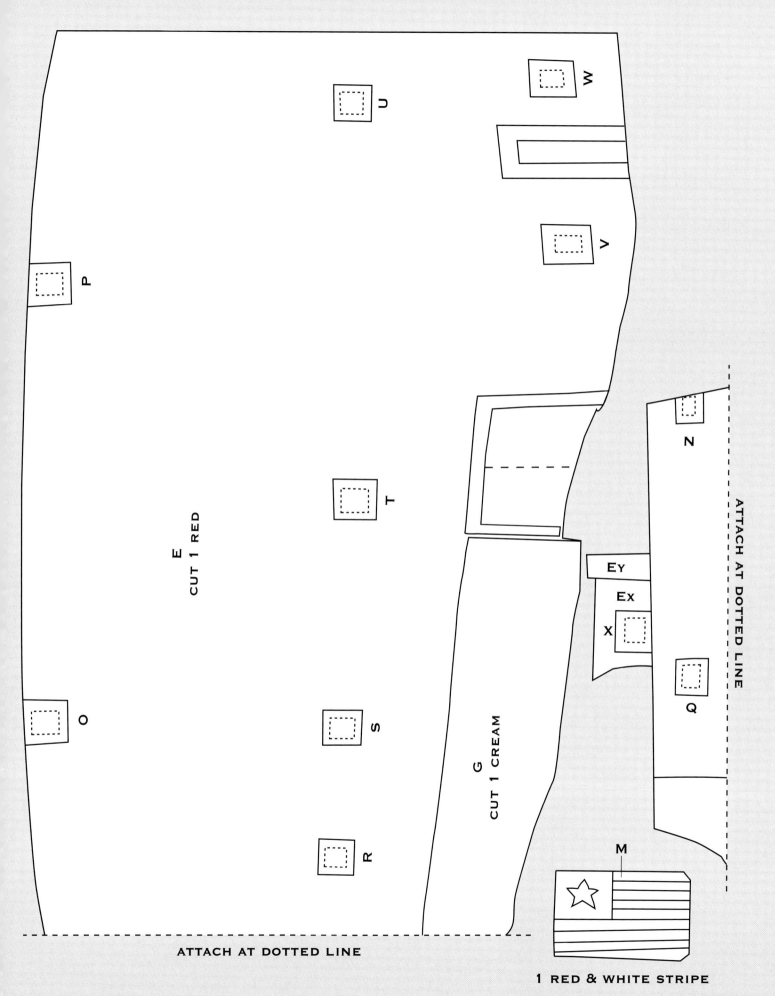

E
CUT 1 RED

G
CUT 1 CREAM

ATTACH AT DOTTED LINE

ATTACH AT DOTTED LINE

W

U

V

P

N

T

O

S

Ey

Ex

X

Q

R

M

1 RED & WHITE STRIPE

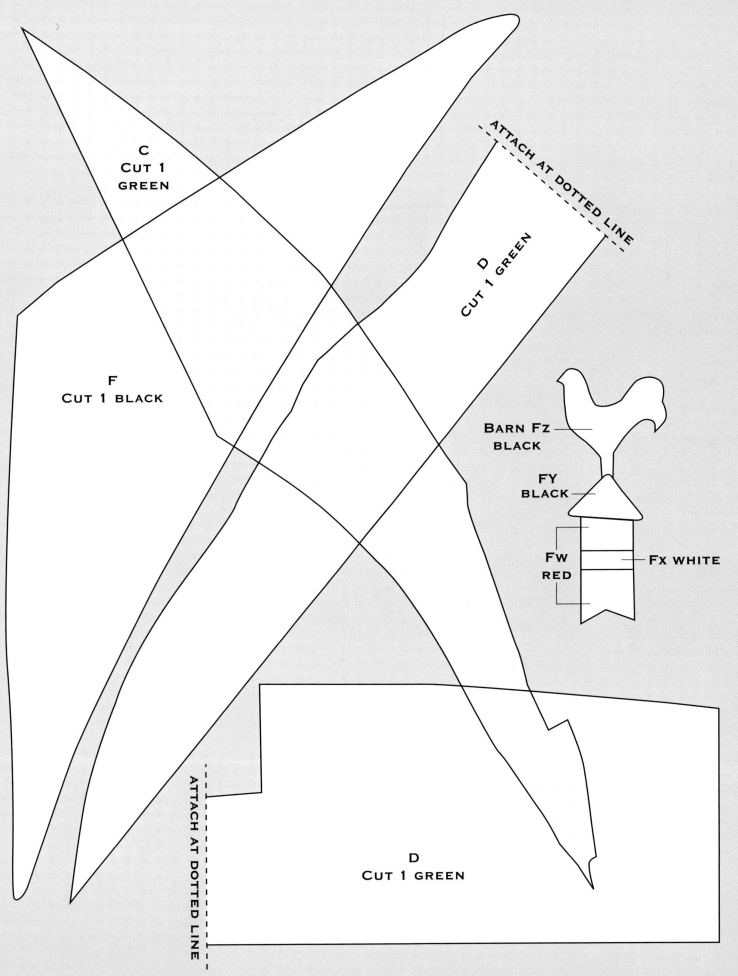

C
Cut 1
green

D
Cut 1 green

ATTACH AT DOTTED LINE

F
Cut 1 black

Barn Fz
black

FY
black

Fw
red

Fx white

ATTACH AT DOTTED LINE

D
Cut 1 green

Add seam allowance on all appliqué pieces when cutting.

L: NINE PATCH
Finished size is 6" x 3".

Fabric Requirement
• Scraps of black and cream checks and patterns

Block Construction
• Cut 3 — 5" x 1 1/2" each of both cream and black scraps.
• Sew together one cream-black-cream set, and one black-cream-black set.
• Square up each end and cut each set into three 1 1/2" x 3 1/2" strips.
• Sew these strips together alternating dark and light as shown.

M: PIGGY
Finished size is 6" x 15".

Fabric Requirements
• One fat 8th or scraps of a cream pattern for the background.
• Scraps of red for the pig and tail
• One 1/2" brown button for eye

Block Construction
• Cut the background 7" x 16".
• For the tail, cut a 1" x 6" strip. Fold the right sides together and sew a 1/4" seam with a basting stitch on your machine. Trim. Turn right side out and draw basting thread so the tail curls into a circle. Attach to the pig as you appliqué the body to the background. Tack the end of the tail to the background. (You could use a 1/4" ribbon instead.)
• For the ear, fold the right sides together and stitch a 1/4" seam, leaving an opening to turn. Turn and press. Fold the longest side in half. Appliqué the ear to the pig by following the stitching lines shown on the pattern. You will sew the left side of the ear in place first, then stitch the right-hand side, leaving a 1/4" space between the two sides. Tack the top of the ear last. The ear will be three-dimensional.
• Attach the eye.
• Trim to 6 1/2" x 15 1/2".

O: LOG CABIN BLOCK
Finished size is 6" x 18".

Fabric Requirements
• Scraps of cream, brown and red stripes and checks

Block Construction
• Cut 3 — 1 1/2" square, red for center.
• Cut 3 — 1 1/2" square, dark.
• Cut 3 — 1 1/2" x 2 1/2" dark rectangles.
• Cut 3 — 1 1/2" x 2 1/2" light rectangles.
• Cut 3 — 1 1/2" x 3 1/2" light rectangles.
• Cut 3 — 1 1/2" x 3 1/2" dark rectangles.
• Cut 3 — 1 1/2" x 4 1/2" dark rectangles.
• Cut 3 — 1 1/2" x 4 1/2" light rectangles.
• Cut 3 — 1 1/2" x 5 1/2" light rectangles.
• Cut 3 — 1 1/2" x 5 1/2" dark rectangles.
• Cut 3 — 1 1/2" x 6 1/2" dark rectangles.
   Assemble into three log cabin blocks and stitch side by side.

P: TREE
Finished size is 16" x 6".

Fabric Requirements
• One fat 8th blue check for background
• One fat 8th brown and tan for trunk
• Scraps of 3 different greens for tree tops

Block Construction
• Cut the background 17" x 7".
• Cut a 16" x 1 7/8" strip for the trunk.
• Appliqué the trunk, and then the tree tops onto the background.
• Trim the block to 16 1/2" x 6 1/2".

Q: HOUSE
Finished size is 16" x 12".

Fabric Requirement
• One fat quarter cream for the background
• One fat 8th red and cream stripe for the house
• Brown scraps for the fireplace
• Black scraps for the roof and windows
• Gold scrap for the star

Block Construction
• Cut the background 17" x 13".
• Line the house up with the bottom of the background and baste into place.
• Appliqué the left side of the house, roof, windows and then the chimney onto the background (Catch the right side windows under the chimney). Add the star. (See picture on page 24 for placement)
• Trim the block to 16 1/2" x 12 1/2".

25

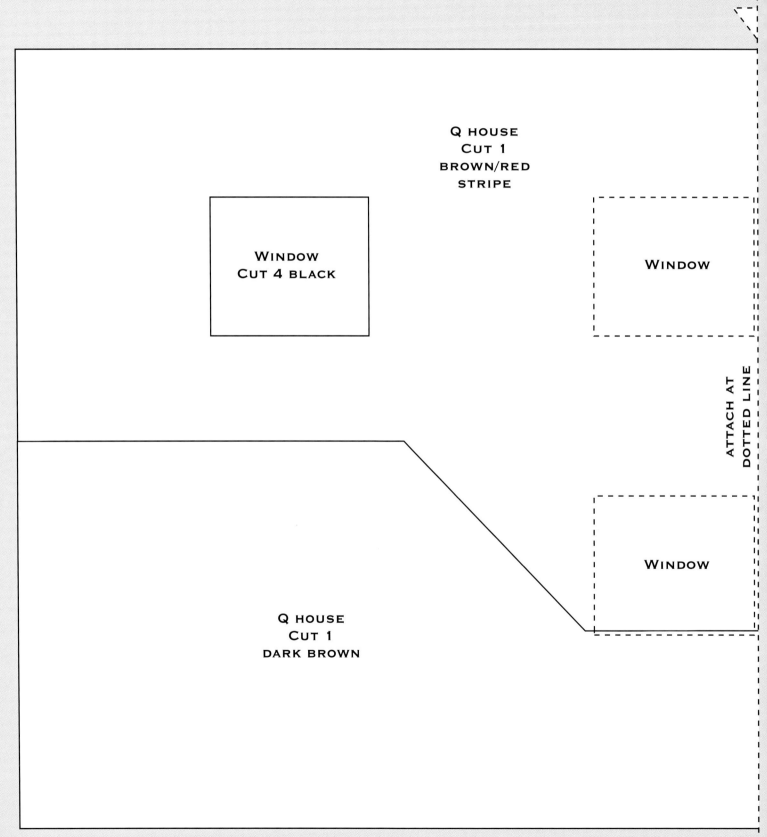

Q HOUSE
CUT 1
BROWN/RED
STRIPE

WINDOW
CUT 4 BLACK

WINDOW

WINDOW

ATTACH AT
DOTTED LINE

Q HOUSE
CUT 1
DARK BROWN

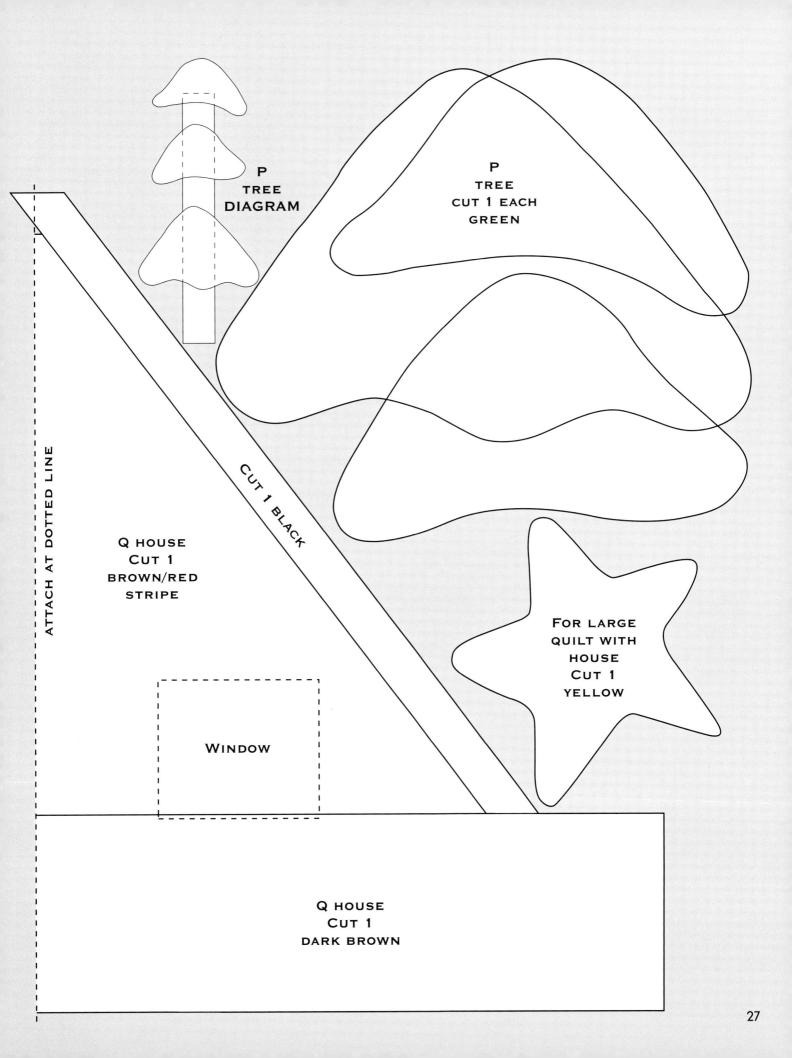

P
TREE
DIAGRAM

P
TREE
CUT 1 EACH
GREEN

ATTACH AT DOTTED LINE

CUT 1 BLACK

Q HOUSE
CUT 1
BROWN/RED
STRIPE

FOR LARGE
QUILT WITH
HOUSE
CUT 1
YELLOW

WINDOW

Q HOUSE
CUT 1
DARK BROWN

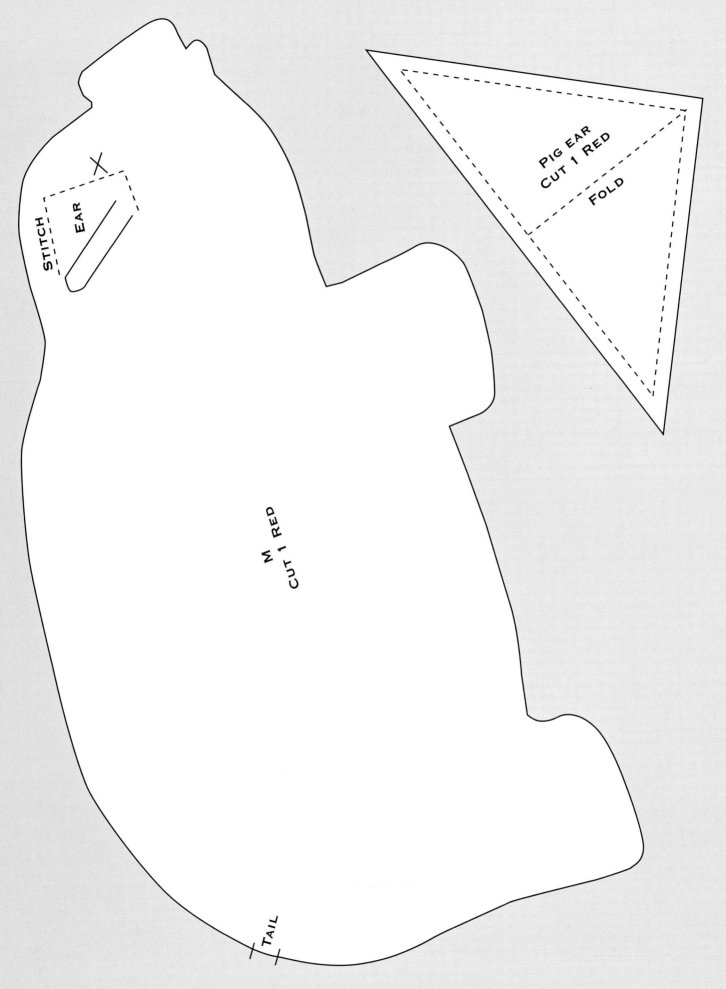

STITCH

EAR

PIG EAR
CUT 1 RED

FOLD

M
CUT 1 RED

TAIL

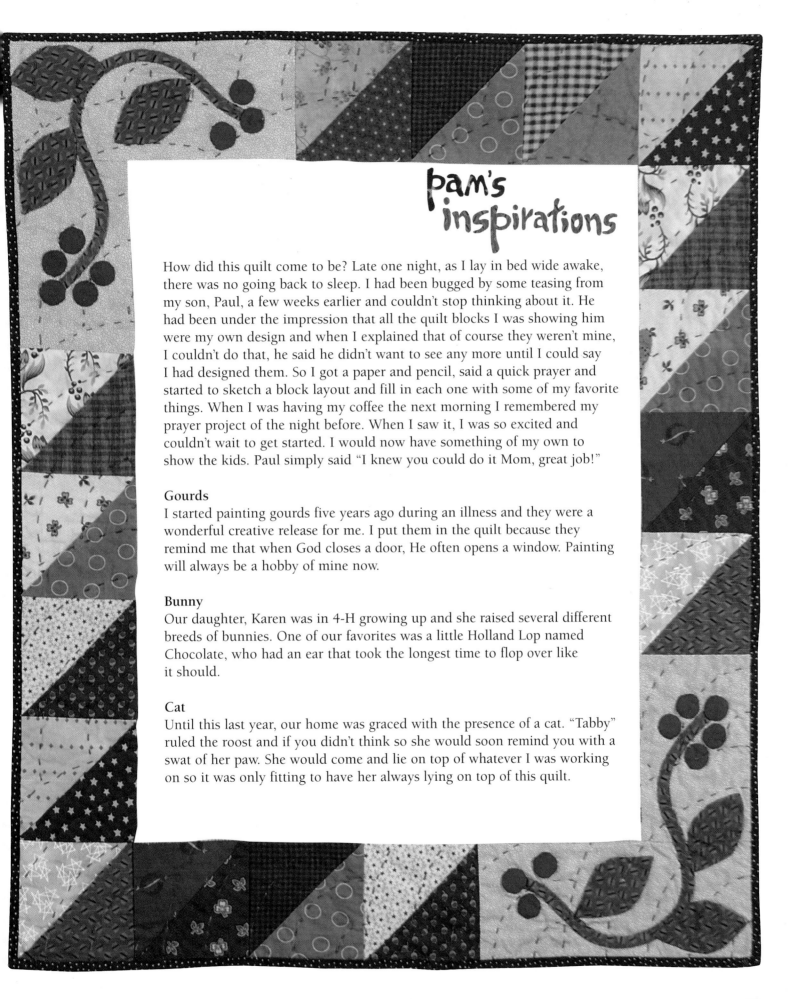

pam's inspirations

How did this quilt come to be? Late one night, as I lay in bed wide awake, there was no going back to sleep. I had been bugged by some teasing from my son, Paul, a few weeks earlier and couldn't stop thinking about it. He had been under the impression that all the quilt blocks I was showing him were my own design and when I explained that of course they weren't mine, I couldn't do that, he said he didn't want to see any more until I could say I had designed them. So I got a paper and pencil, said a quick prayer and started to sketch a block layout and fill in each one with some of my favorite things. When I was having my coffee the next morning I remembered my prayer project of the night before. When I saw it, I was so excited and couldn't wait to get started. I would now have something of my own to show the kids. Paul simply said "I knew you could do it Mom, great job!"

Gourds
I started painting gourds five years ago during an illness and they were a wonderful creative release for me. I put them in the quilt because they remind me that when God closes a door, He often opens a window. Painting will always be a hobby of mine now.

Bunny
Our daughter, Karen was in 4-H growing up and she raised several different breeds of bunnies. One of our favorites was a little Holland Lop named Chocolate, who had an ear that took the longest time to flop over like it should.

Cat
Until this last year, our home was graced with the presence of a cat. "Tabby" ruled the roost and if you didn't think so she would soon remind you with a swat of her paw. She would come and lie on top of whatever I was working on so it was only fitting to have her always lying on top of this quilt.

Add seam allowance on all appliqué pieces when cutting.

N: RAIL FENCE
Finished size is 5" x 2".

Fabric Requirements
• Four scraps of rust, blue, green and tan check

Block Construction
A: Cut 1 green and tan check — 1 1/2" x 2 1/2".
B- Cut 1 rust — 1 1/4" x 6".
C- Cut 2 blue — 1 1/8" x 6".
Sandwich the B strip (rust) between the two C strips (blue) and sew lengthwise. Trim and cut to 2 1/2" lengths. Press seams all one way. Join the ends together with the A green/tan check between them.

W: FLYING GEESE
Finished size is 2" x 16".

Fabric Requirements
• Scraps of creams for the geese
• Red, navy and cream check for the outside pieces

Block Construction
• Cut 4 — 3 1/4" light squares.
• Cut 16 — 1 7/8" darker squares.
• Follow the directions for A in the green section on page 7.
• Assemble in a row and point your geese in the same direction.

R: TREES
Finished block size is 23" x 8".

Fabric Requirement
• One fat quarter or scraps of tan and small blue/cream check for the background (Remember, piecing looks great for primitive and folk art projects.) or use a piece from which you can get 24".
• Brown and tan scraps for trunks
• Scraps of various greens for tree tops

Block Construction
• Cut background 24" x 9".
• Appliqué the tall tree on the right of the block. Save the small tree for when you have combined the purple and orange sections. Then you will appliqué on the joining line.
• Trim block to 23 1/2" x 8 1/2".

T: LARGE GOURD
Finished block size is 11" x 10".

Fabric Requirement
• One fat 8th of gold and red check for background
• One fat 8th or scraps of dark brown for gourd
• Scraps of green for the stem, and black scraps for the hole

Block Construction
• Cut background 12" x 11".
• Appliqué to the background.
• Trim block to 11 1/2" x 10 1/2".

U: 10 SQUARE ROW
Finished block size is 1" x 10".

Fabric Requirement
• Scraps of tan, black and black and tan check

Block Construction
• Cut 5 — 1 1/2" square tan or light color.
• Cut 5 — 1 1/2" square black or dark color.
• Sew alternating colors to form your 10" finished strip.

V: DAISIES IN A PAIL
Finished block size is 11" x 10".

Fabric Requirement
• One fat quarter brown, tan and cream plaid for background,
• Scraps of gray for pail, dark green for stems, and varied greens for leaves
• Bleached muslin for flower petals
• Black 8-strand floss

Block Construction
• Cut background 12" x 11".
• Cut stems 33" x 1 1/4" on the diagonal. Fold wrong sides together and stitch 1/4" from raw edge lengthwise. Trim to 1/8". Insert a 1/4" press rod and press the seam to the middle of the back of the stem. (For stems that have to bend over the bucket, I run a basting thread along the edge and gather it up before I appliqué, removing it when I am done).
• Glue pieces to be appliquéd in place with dots of glue.
• Appliqué the back of the pail, then the stems and bucket base.
• Add the flower circles, petals, leaves and handle.
• Embroider the wire handle with black floss.
• Trim block to 11 1/2" x 10 1/2".

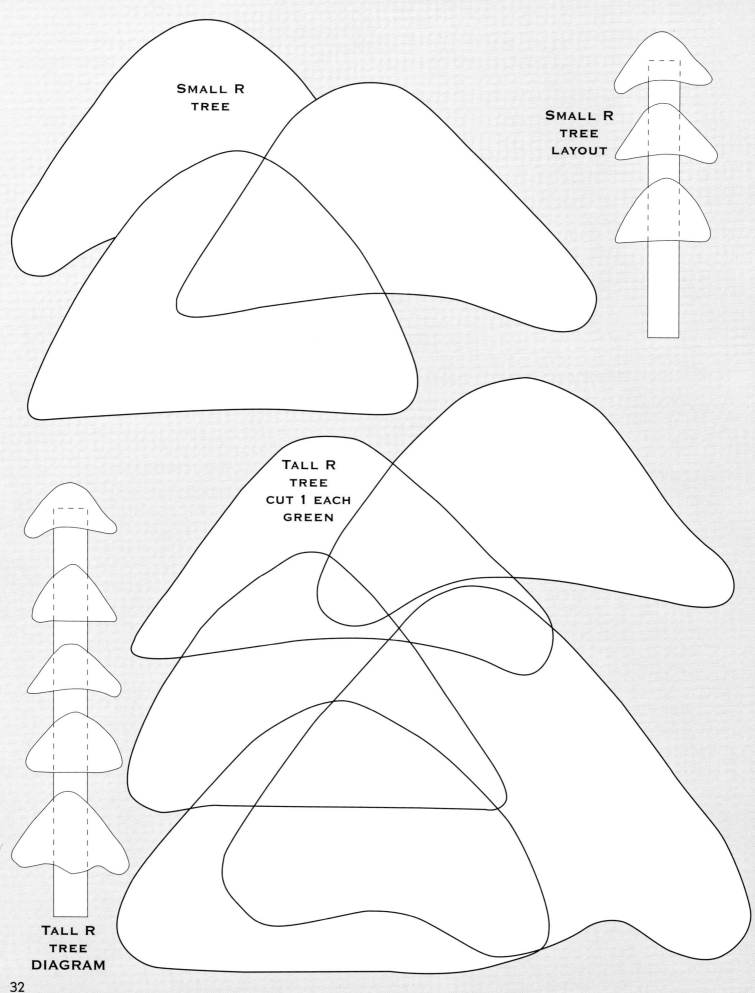

SMALL R
TREE

SMALL R
TREE
LAYOUT

TALL R
TREE
CUT 1 EACH
GREEN

TALL R
TREE
DIAGRAM

32

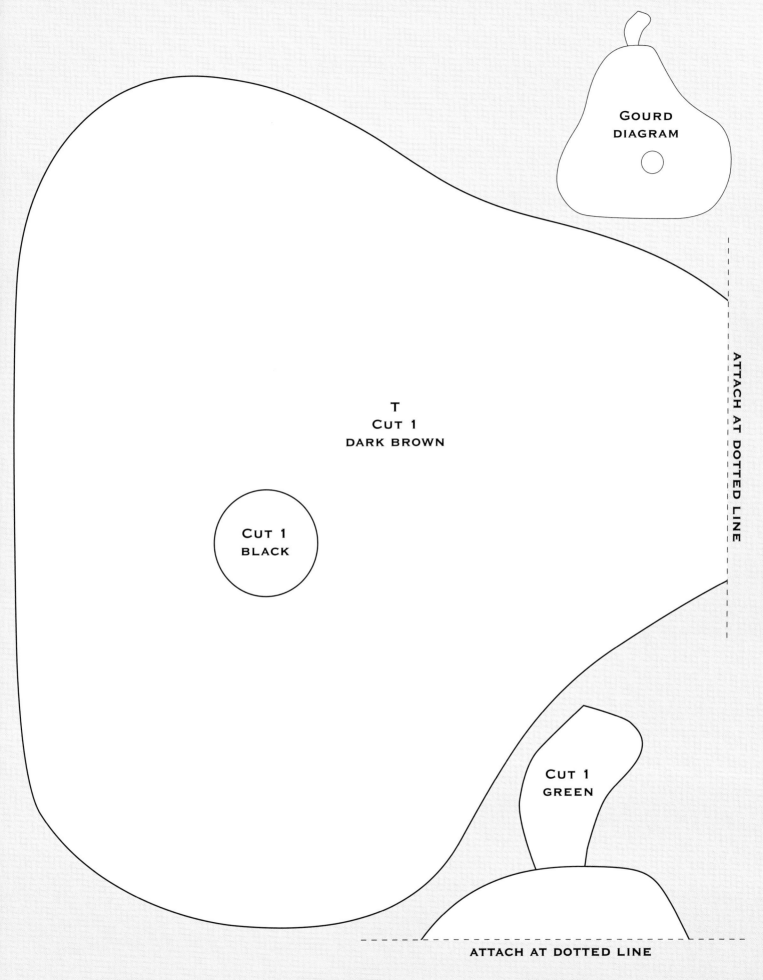

GOURD
DIAGRAM

T
CUT 1
DARK BROWN

CUT 1
BLACK

CUT 1
GREEN

ATTACH AT DOTTED LINE

ATTACH AT DOTTED LINE

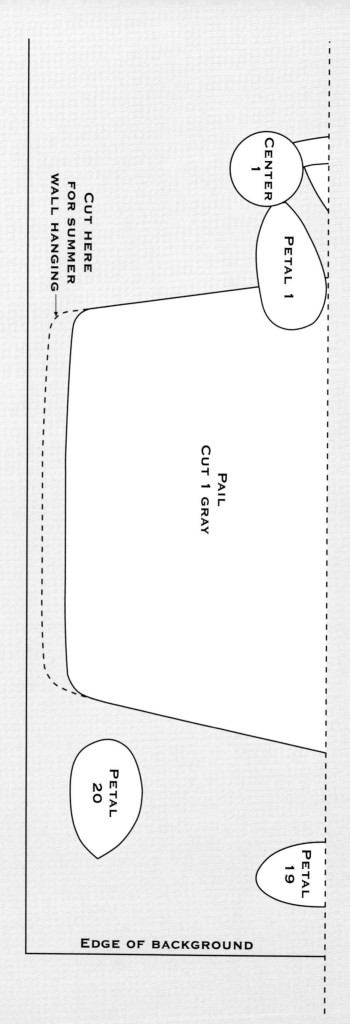

CENTER 1

PETAL 1

PAIL
CUT 1 GRAY

CUT HERE
FOR SUMMER
WALL HANGING

PETAL 20

PETAL 19

EDGE OF BACKGROUND

34

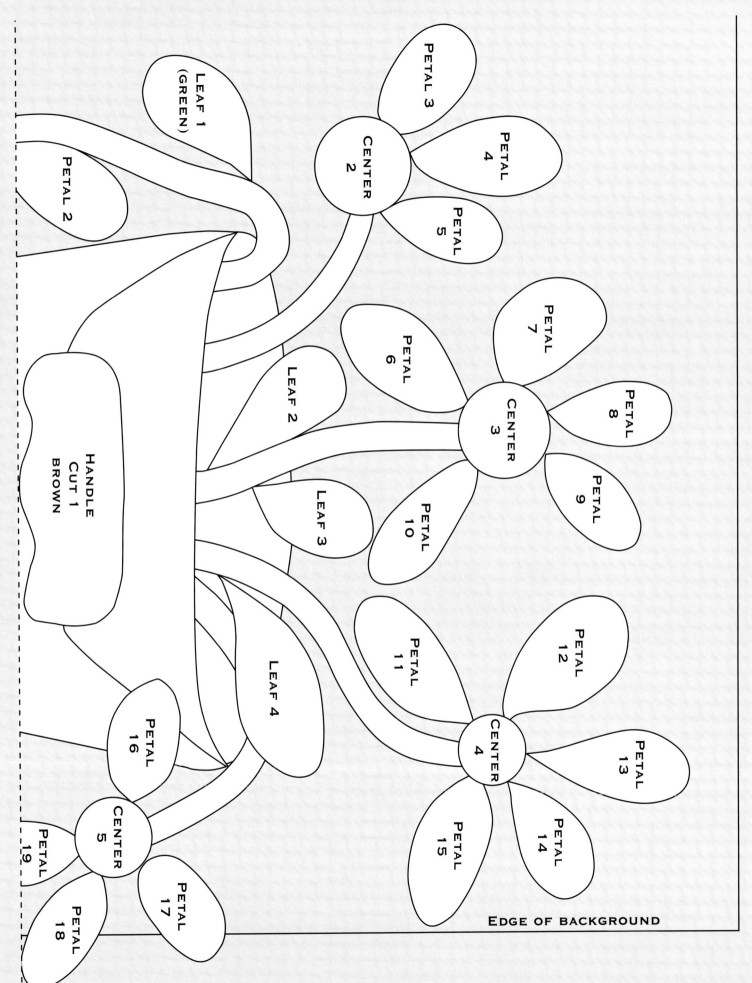

PETAL 3

PETAL 4

PETAL 5

CENTER 2

LEAF 1 (GREEN)

PETAL 2

PETAL 7

PETAL 6

PETAL 8

CENTER 3

PETAL 9

LEAF 2

PETAL 10

HANDLE CUT 1 BROWN

LEAF 3

PETAL 12

PETAL 11

LEAF 4

CENTER 4

PETAL 13

PETAL 15

PETAL 14

PETAL 16

CENTER 5

PETAL 19

PETAL 17

PETAL 18

EDGE OF BACKGROUND

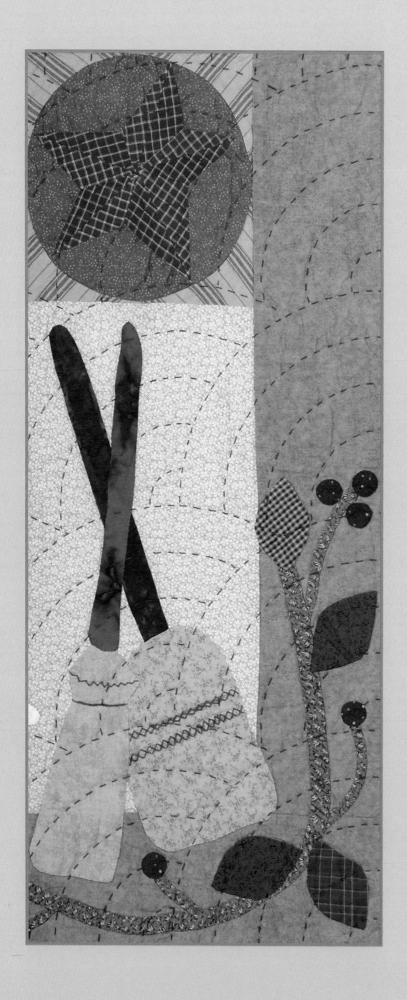

Add seam allowance on all appliqué pieces when cutting.

X: CIRCLE WITH SET-IN STAR
Finished size is 8" x 8".

Fabric Requirements
• Scraps of gold and red stripe for the background
• Red and cream check, and brown and cream check for the star

Block Construction
This is probably the hardest block for anyone not familiar with piecing much, but go ahead and try it. Sometimes we surprise ourselves! If you hate it, use the circle and star pattern and appliqué this block. But keep smiling!
• To piece the block, cut S, R, Q & P with seam allowance from the gold and red stripe. If not piecing, cut one 8 1/2" square for background.
• Cut pieces B, E, H, K, and N in red and cream check, adding 1/4" seam allowance.
• Cut pieces A, D, G, J, and M in brown and cream check, adding 1/4" seam allowance.
• Be sure to press your seams as you go, keeping everything flat. Trim seams where the inside points come together to avoid bulking. Freezer paper piecing is good for this project as it helps to keep track of where each piece fits in. Transfer your marks for all pattern pieces as this will help you when you start assembling your block.
• Join A to B, D to E, G to H, J to K, M to N to seam allowance (leave seam allowance open).
• Join AB to C, DE to F, GH to I, KJ to L, and NM to O.
• Join B to D, E to G, H to J, K to M, N to A. Your circle is now complete. If you have had enough at this point you can appliqué your circle to a full 8 1/2" square unfinished and you're done.
• If you opt for more piecing, sew the pieces S to R, R to Q, Q to P and P to S at the seam allowance. Clip the inside curves of S, R, Q and P.
• Now line up your marks, pinning around the whole circle. Work with the outside pieces S, R, Q, and P on top as your feed dog will help gather the circle below.
• Press.

Y: BROOMS
Finished size is 17" x 8".

Fabric Requirements
• One fat quarter cream and tan for the background
• Scraps of 2 golds for the brooms
• Scraps of 2 browns for the handles

Block Construction
• Cut background 18" x 7".
• Appliqué the brooms on, letting them hang over the edge of the block as illustrated on the pattern. You will appliqué these on the border when it is added.
• Trim block to 17 1/2" x 8 1/2".

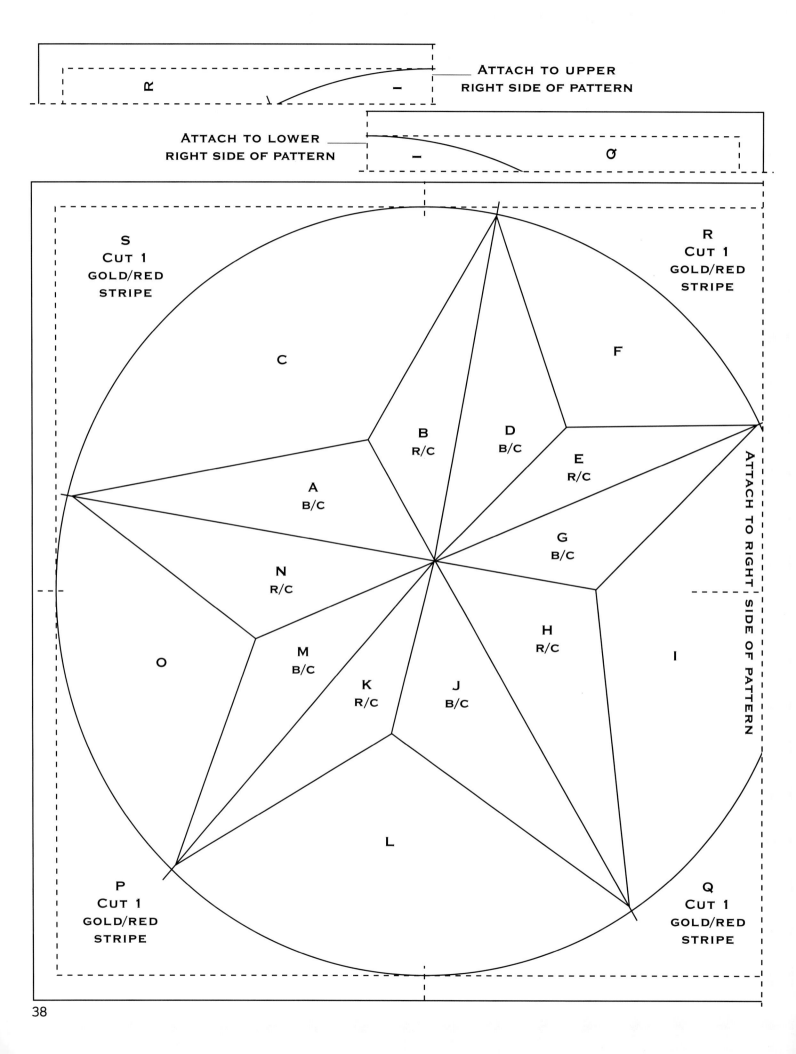

ATTACH TO UPPER
RIGHT SIDE OF PATTERN

R

ATTACH TO LOWER
RIGHT SIDE OF PATTERN

σ

S
CUT 1
GOLD/RED
STRIPE

R
CUT 1
GOLD/RED
STRIPE

C

F

B
R/C

D
B/C

E
R/C

A
B/C

G
B/C

N
R/C

ATTACH TO RIGHT SIDE OF PATTERN

O

M
B/C

H
R/C

I

K
R/C

J
B/C

L

P
CUT 1
GOLD/RED
STRIPE

Q
CUT 1
GOLD/RED
STRIPE

38

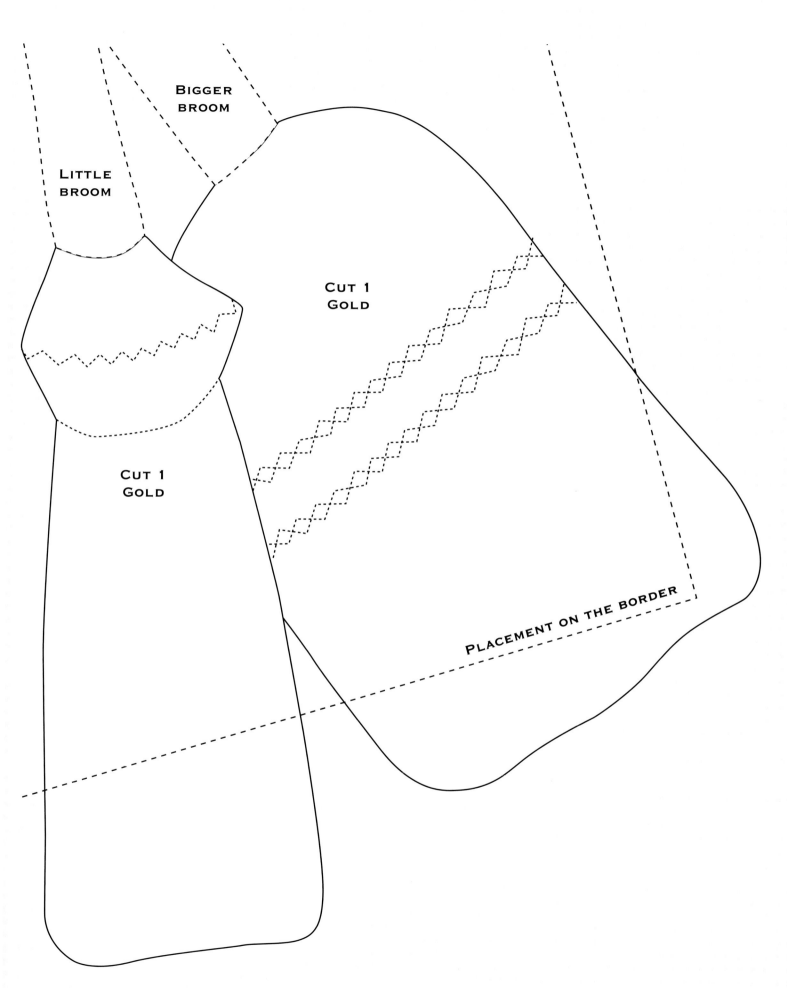

LITTLE
BROOM

BIGGER
BROOM

CUT 1
GOLD

CUT 1
GOLD

PLACEMENT ON THE BORDER

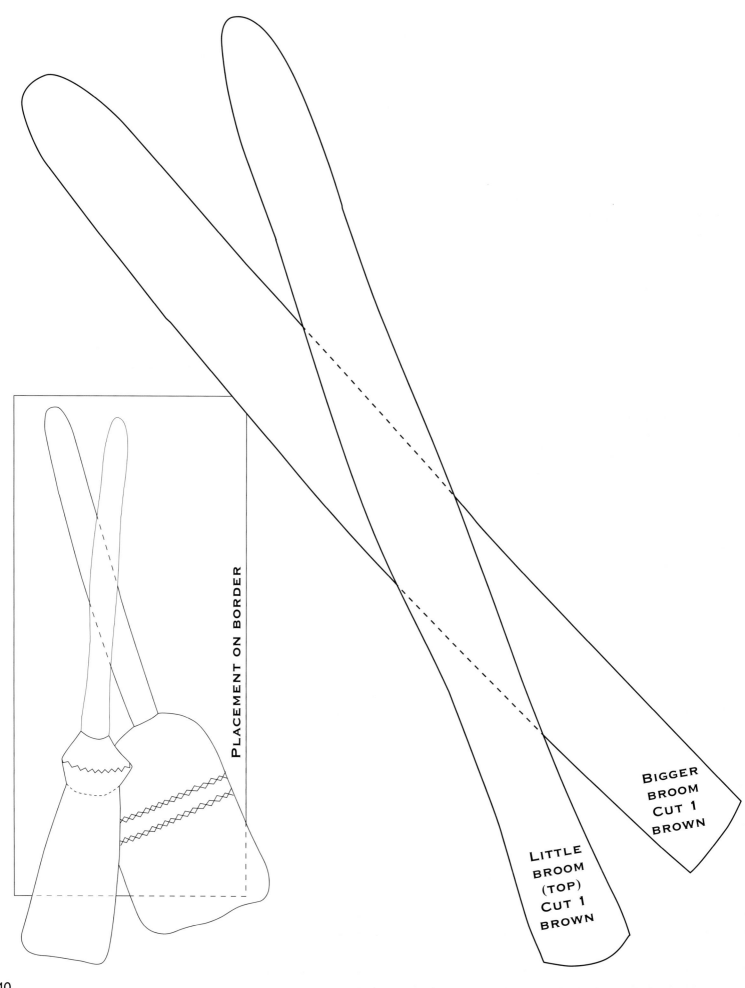

PLACEMENT ON BORDER

LITTLE
broom
(TOP)
CUT 1
brown

BIGGER
broom
CUT 1
brown

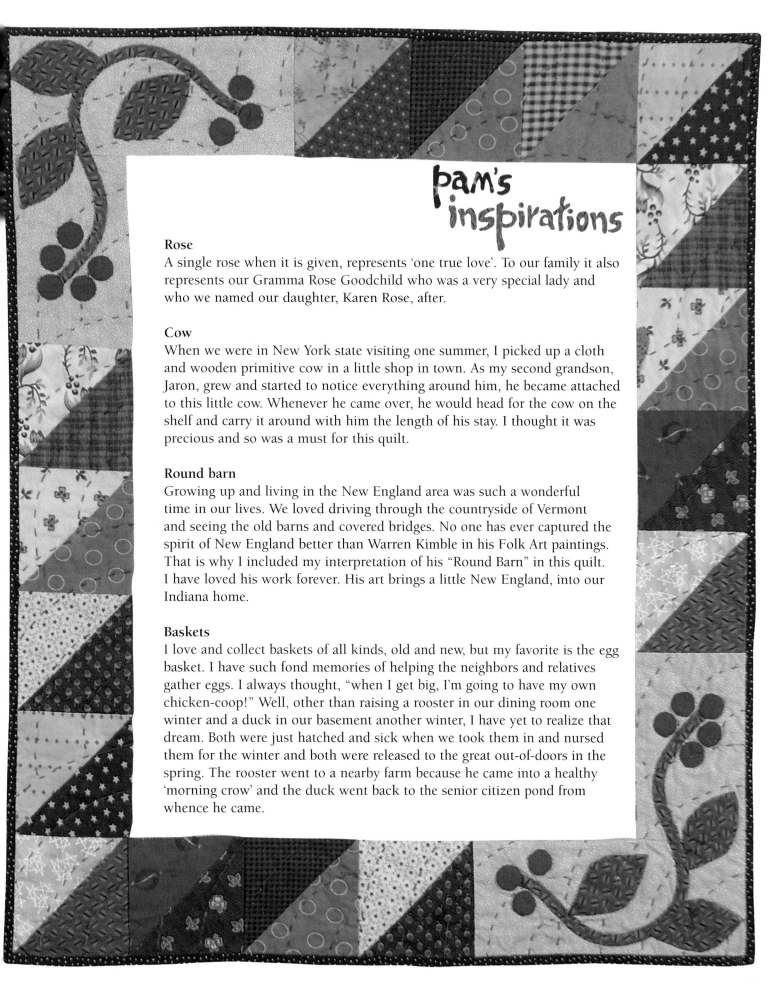

pam's inspirations

Rose

A single rose when it is given, represents 'one true love'. To our family it also represents our Gramma Rose Goodchild who was a very special lady and who we named our daughter, Karen Rose, after.

Cow

When we were in New York state visiting one summer, I picked up a cloth and wooden primitive cow in a little shop in town. As my second grandson, Jaron, grew and started to notice everything around him, he became attached to this little cow. Whenever he came over, he would head for the cow on the shelf and carry it around with him the length of his stay. I thought it was precious and so was a must for this quilt.

Round barn

Growing up and living in the New England area was such a wonderful time in our lives. We loved driving through the countryside of Vermont and seeing the old barns and covered bridges. No one has ever captured the spirit of New England better than Warren Kimble in his Folk Art paintings. That is why I included my interpretation of his "Round Barn" in this quilt. I have loved his work forever. His art brings a little New England, into our Indiana home.

Baskets

I love and collect baskets of all kinds, old and new, but my favorite is the egg basket. I have such fond memories of helping the neighbors and relatives gather eggs. I always thought, "when I get big, I'm going to have my own chicken-coop!" Well, other than raising a rooster in our dining room one winter and a duck in our basement another winter, I have yet to realize that dream. Both were just hatched and sick when we took them in and nursed them for the winter and both were released to the great out-of-doors in the spring. The rooster went to a nearby farm because he came into a healthy 'morning crow' and the duck went back to the senior citizen pond from whence he came.

JOINING YOUR SECTIONS

1. GREEN SECTION:
Join A to B
Join A, B to C
JoinABC to D
Join E and F
Join EF to bottom of CD

2. BLUE SECTION:
Join G to H
Join I to J
Join GH to IJ
Join K to IJ

3. ORANGE SECTION:
Join L to M
Join O set to LM
Join P to Q
Join PQ to bottom of O set

4. PURPLE SECTION:
Join N to W
Join T to U and U to V
Join TUV to R
Join NW to top of RT

5. AQUA SECTION:
Join X to Y
Join XY to WTUV

6. RED SECTION:
Join Za to Aa
Join Aa side to Zb

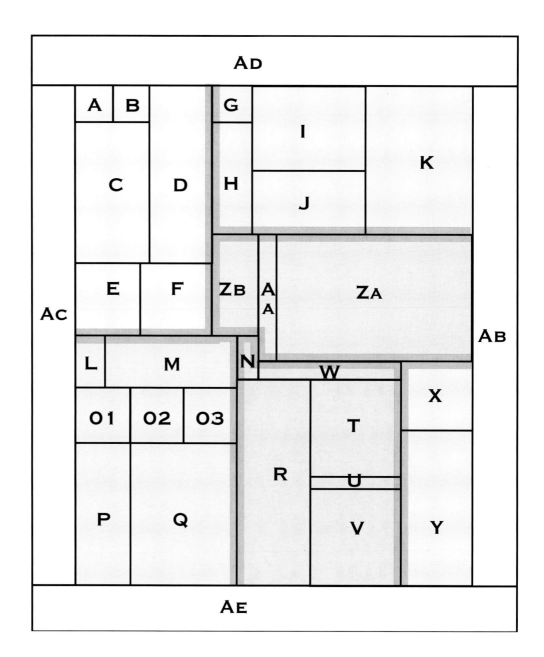

42

- Stitch blocks together into sections as shown.
- See the chart on page 42 for joining the SIX SECTIONS together as follows.
Press your seams as you progress.
- Join blocks HJK (the bottom blocks of the (BLUE SECTION) to the top of ZbAaZa (your RED SECTION).
- Join the right side of DF to GHZb.
- Join the left side of XY (AQUA SECTION) to the right side of WTUV (PURPLE SECTION).
- Join the left side of NR (PURPLE SECTION) to MOQ (ORANGE SECTION).
- Join the bottom of EFZbAaZa to the top of LMNWX.
- Join the right side of N to the left side of Aa.

BORDER
Finished size is 5" wide.

Fabric Requirements
- 1/2 yard of light tan
- 1/2 yard of darker tan

Border Construction
- Cut 3—5 1/2" widths of each fabric.
- Make one strip of dark tan (Ab) 5 1/2" x 56 1/2".
- Make one strip of dark tan (Ae) 5 1/2" x 54 1/2".
- Make one strip of light tan (Ac) 5 1/2" x 56 1/2".
- Make one strip of light tan (Ad) 5 1/2" x 54 1/2".
- Attach the sides (Ab) and (Ac) first and then the top (Ad) and bottom (Ae).
- Appliqué the bottom of the brooms onto the border.

VINES & BERRIES

Fabric Requirements
- One 1/2 yard green for the 3/8" vine and 7/8" vine.
- Six different green scrap pieces for leaves
- One fat 8th red for berries

Construction
- Cut 6 leaves from each of five greens and 4 from the last green, 34 leaves in all.
- You will need to cut 5 yards by 2 1/4" green on the diagonal from the green fabric for the 7/8" vines. Join your pieces with a diagonal seam.
- Cut 2 1/2 yards by 1 1/4" green cut on the diagonal for the 3/8" stems, joining pieces with a diagonal seam.
- Fold the wrong sides of the 2 1/4" vine together lengthwise and stitch a 1/4" seam.
- Fold the wrong sides together of the 1 1/4" vine lengthwise and stitch a 1/4" seam.
- Trim the seam. Insert a 1/2" press bar, roll the seam to one side and press. Remove the bar and press again. Use a 3/8" press bar for the stems and repeat.
- Pin or glue the vine in place as in the photo, adding stems in appropriate places. Appliqué in place.
- Finish with the berries. You will need 61 berries the size of a penny. You can trace them on freezer paper, cut and iron them on the wrong side of your fabric. Cut out, adding a 1/4" seam and then baste around the outside edge and draw it around forming a berry. You can spray them with starch and press them.
- Appliqué them on, pulling the paper out just before you finish the last inch of appliqué.

FINISHING YOUR QUILT
Finished size is 66" x 54".

Do something creative to make your quilt back interesting and creative. Be sure to at least date and initial your quilt. Use a good cotton batting such as Hobb's Heirloom Cotton.

Remember — you always want your back to be at least 4 - 5" bigger than your front for quilting.

Ed. note: See the back of Pam's quilt on back cover.

Add seam allowance on all appliqué pieces when cutting.

Finished size is 25 1/2" x 29 1/4".

Fabric Requirements
- One fat quarter brown check for background
- Scraps of pink or wine for the bunny
- Scraps of four greens for the tree and leaves
- Scraps of cream for the letters
- Scraps of purple and wines for the eggs
- Scraps for the border (charm packs work great for this kind of border)
- 3/4 yard for backing

Block Construction
- Cut a 19" x 22 3/4" rectangle for the center block.
- Appliqué bunny, tree, letters and eggs in place.
- Trim the center to 18" x 21 3/4".
- Cut 7 - 1 3/4" x 7 1/2" rectangles from each of nine different fabrics for the four 9-patches for the corners (See directions for 9-patch on page 25.)
- Sew three fabric strips together until you have three sets of three strips.
- Square up your first end, cut into strips 1 3/4" wide, and toss the end piece. Assemble your four 9-patch blocks. (They will all have nine different fabrics in them and measure 4 1/2" at this point.)
- Cut 14 fabrics 1 3/4" x 17 1/2". Sew together lengthwise. Press in the same direction.
- Cut into 4 - 4 1/2" strips.
- Cut three fabrics 1 3/4" x 9". Sew lengthwise and cut into two 4 1/2" strips.
- Add one to each of two of the long strips. Press.
- Sew the long strips onto the sides.
- Add the 9-patch to each end of remaining strips and add these strips to the top and the bottom of the wall hanging.

To Finish
- Add the cotton batting and backing. Big-stitch and bind. Date and sign your work.

Bunny template on p. 9
Letters template on p. 17

45

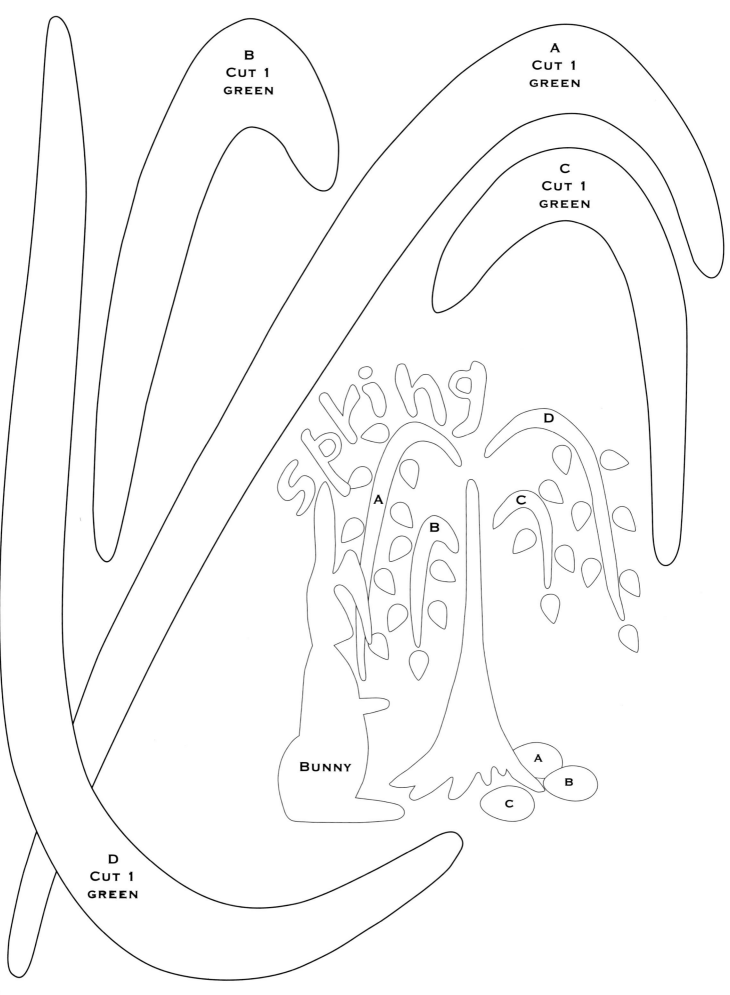

B
Cut 1
green

A
Cut 1
green

C
Cut 1
green

spring

D

A

C

B

Bunny

A

B

C

D
Cut 1
green

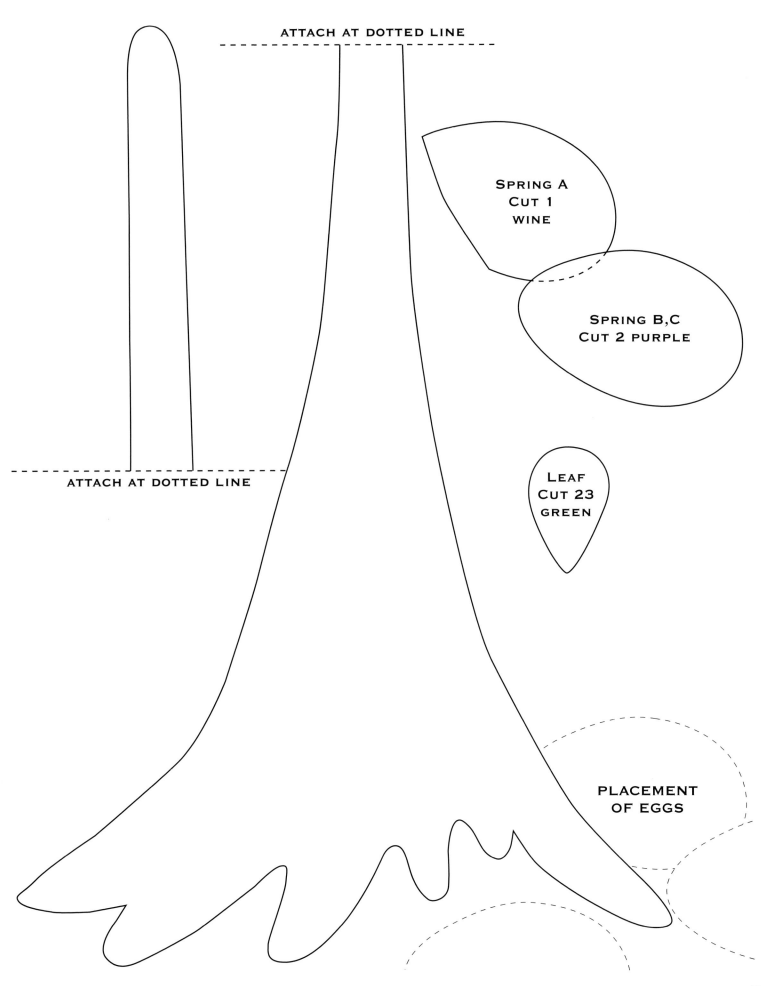

ATTACH AT DOTTED LINE

Spring A
Cut 1
wine

Spring B,C
Cut 2 purple

Leaf
Cut 23
green

ATTACH AT DOTTED LINE

PLACEMENT
OF EGGS

Add seam allowance on all appliqué pieces when cutting.

Finished size is 26" x 30 3/4".

Fabric Requirement
- 8 fat sixteenths or scraps cream for background
- Scraps for pattern pieces of black, red, gray, green, gold/red, 3 browns, 2 golds and brown and black plaid
- 8 - 5" squares of assorted dark fabrics and 8 - 5" squares of assorted light fabrics for the border
- One fat quarter tan fabric for border corners
- One fat quarter red for the pump
- 3/4 yard for backing

Block Construction

Center block
The center block is made up of eight blocks, finishing 17 1/2" x 22 1/4".
- Cut one block 4 3/4" x 10 1/2" and one 4 3/4" x 8 1/2". Join the short edges.
- Cut six 6 1/2" x 9 3/4" rectangles. Sew together two sets of three blocks stitched lengthwise.
- Join these two sections with short ends of blocks together and add the two-block section to the top.
- Appliqué pieces in place, starting with the base of the well, then the pump. Add the brooms, large, then small. Add the bucket, (leaving room to tuck in the back of the pail and the stems of the flowers). Appliqué stems, petals, centers and leaves, spreading them out a little more and making the flower stems a little longer than on the quilt. Add the handle and embroider the wire of the handle using a stem stitch.
- Trim the center block to 18" x 22 3/4".

Border
- For the half-square triangles, cut eight lighter blocks 5" square and eight darker blocks 5" square.
- Draw a diagonal line from the top corner to the opposite bottom corner of the light squares.
- Place one dark and one light square right sides together and sew a seam 1/4" on each side of the diagonal line.

- Cut on the line with your rotary cutter. Press the seam open to the dark side.
- Trim the block to 4 1/2" square. You will now have 16 blocks.
- Cut two rectangles 10" x 4 1/2" and two rectangles 6 3/4" x 4 1/2".
- Join two sets of four blocks each (tops to bottoms) and add a 6 3/4"x 4 1/2" rectangle to the bottom for the right-side strip and to the top for the left-side strip. Join these strips to the center block. Keep the dark side on half-square triangles going in the same direction.
- Make two more sets of four blocks each and add a 10" x 4 1/2" rectangle to the left side for the top row and to the right side for the bottom row.
- Attach to the wall hanging.
- Appliqué the stem, berries and leaves on the solid colored corners following the pattern diagram.

To Finish
- Add the cotton batting and backing. Big-stitch and bind. Date and sign your work.

Pail template on pp. 34 and 35
Letters template on p. 17

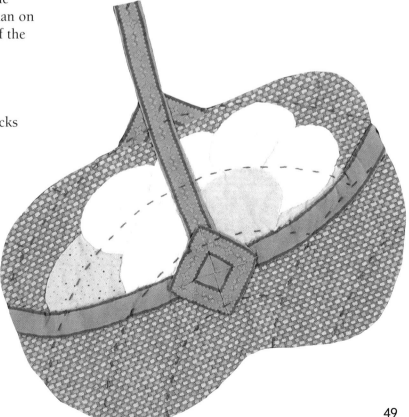

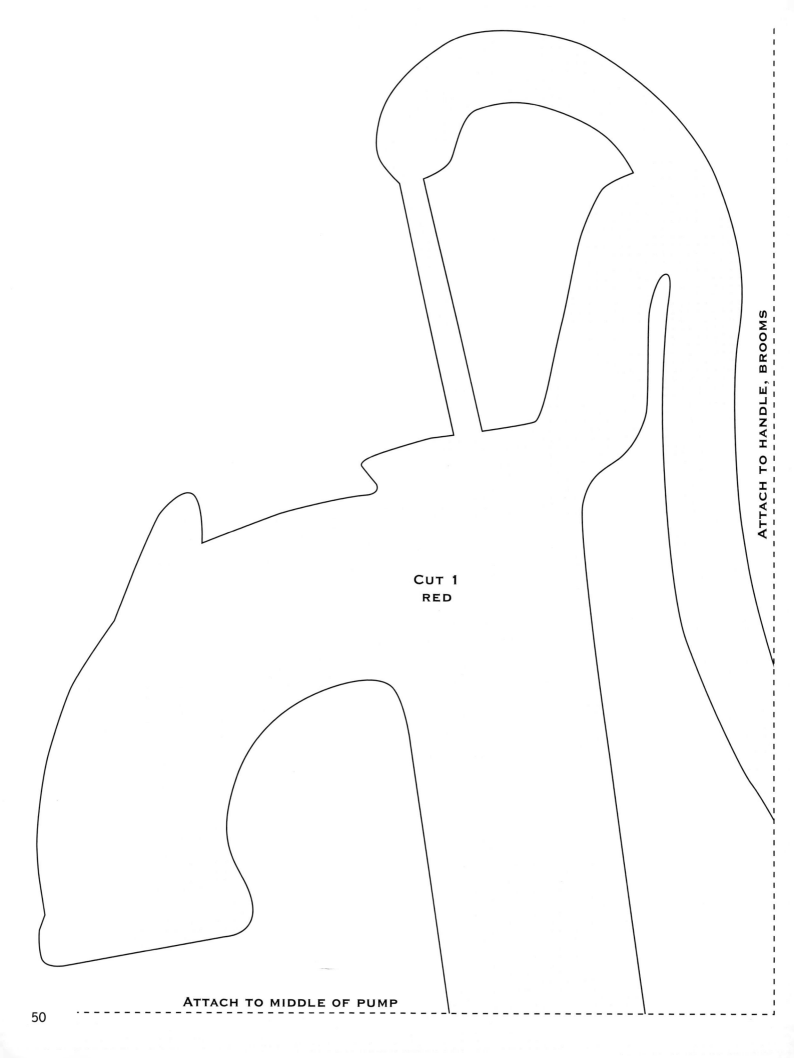

CUT 1
RED

ATTACH TO HANDLE, BROOMS

ATTACH TO MIDDLE OF PUMP

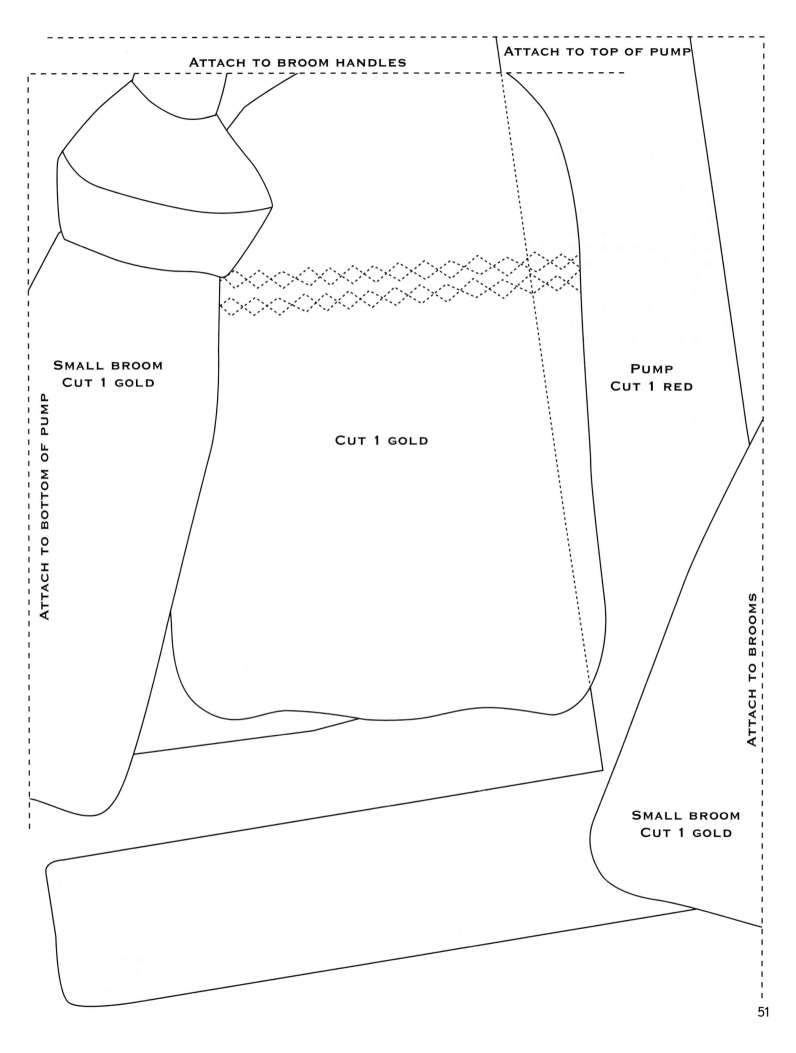

ATTACH TO BROOM HANDLES

ATTACH TO TOP OF PUMP

SMALL BROOM
CUT 1 GOLD

PUMP
CUT 1 RED

ATTACH TO BOTTOM OF PUMP

CUT 1 GOLD

ATTACH TO BROOMS

SMALL BROOM
CUT 1 GOLD

51

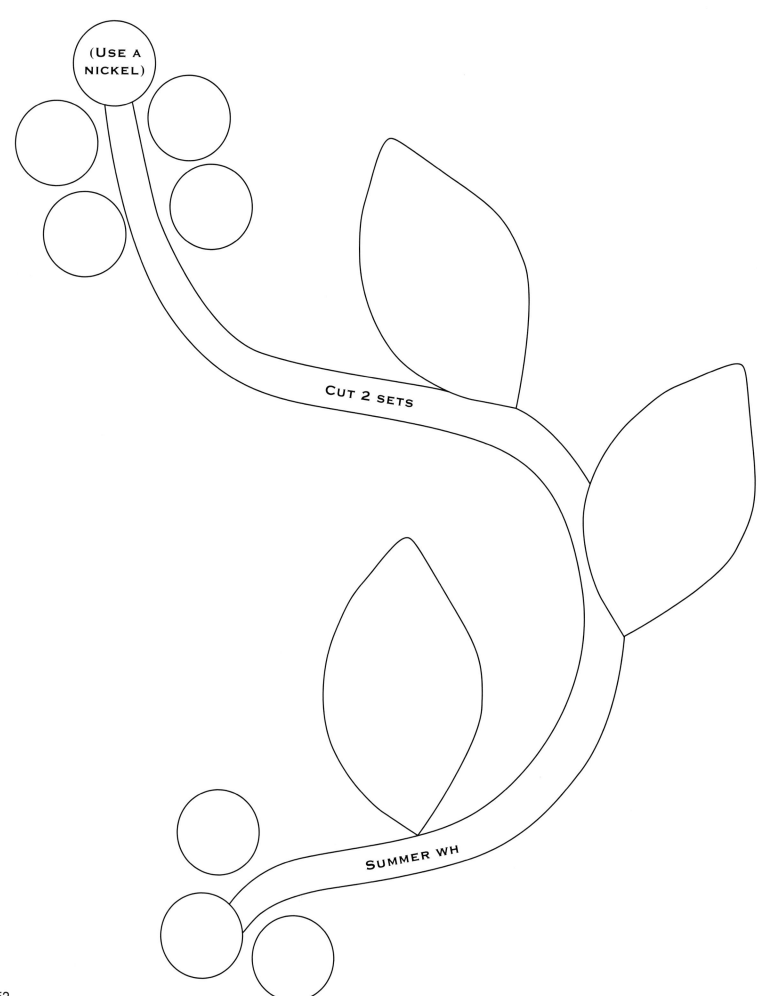

(Use a
nickel)

Cut 2 sets

Summer wh

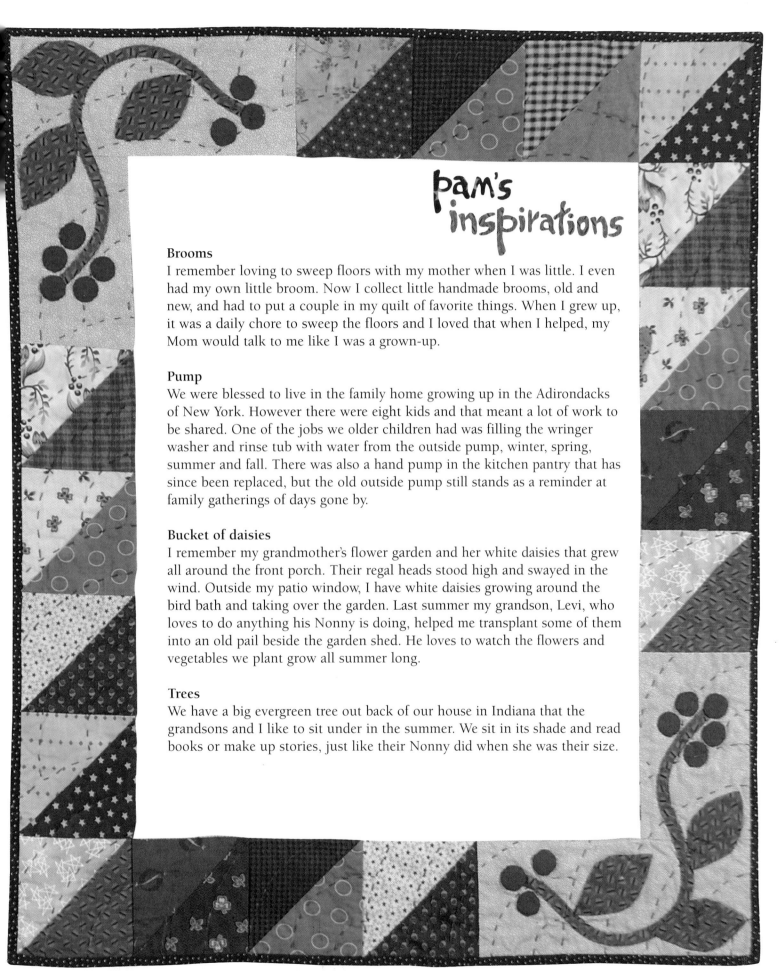

pam's inspirations

Brooms
I remember loving to sweep floors with my mother when I was little. I even had my own little broom. Now I collect little handmade brooms, old and new, and had to put a couple in my quilt of favorite things. When I grew up, it was a daily chore to sweep the floors and I loved that when I helped, my Mom would talk to me like I was a grown-up.

Pump
We were blessed to live in the family home growing up in the Adirondacks of New York. However there were eight kids and that meant a lot of work to be shared. One of the jobs we older children had was filling the wringer washer and rinse tub with water from the outside pump, winter, spring, summer and fall. There was also a hand pump in the kitchen pantry that has since been replaced, but the old outside pump still stands as a reminder at family gatherings of days gone by.

Bucket of daisies
I remember my grandmother's flower garden and her white daisies that grew all around the front porch. Their regal heads stood high and swayed in the wind. Outside my patio window, I have white daisies growing around the bird bath and taking over the garden. Last summer my grandson, Levi, who loves to do anything his Nonny is doing, helped me transplant some of them into an old pail beside the garden shed. He loves to watch the flowers and vegetables we plant grow all summer long.

Trees
We have a big evergreen tree out back of our house in Indiana that the grandsons and I like to sit under in the summer. We sit in its shade and read books or make up stories, just like their Nonny did when she was their size.

Add seam allowance on all appliqué pieces when cutting.

Finished size is 26 1/4" x 30".

Fabric Requirements
• 2/3 yard cream and light blue stripe for background
• Scrap of orange and brown for the large gourd
• Scrap of cream for the small gourd
• Scrap of light and dark brown for the long handled gourd
• Scrap of black for the crow
• Scraps of green plaid, brown, and red with white stars
• Scraps of three mixed greens for stems and leaves
• Scrap of red for berries
• Scraps of 16 different fabrics in colors you like. I used golds, reds, black, greens, blue, browns and gray.
• 3/4 yard for backing

Block Construction
• Cut the center block 21 3/4" x 25 1/2".
• Cut 18 1/2" x 1 3/4" of green on the diagonal. This will be the (5/8") vine.
• Cut 17" x 1 1/4" of the same green on the diagonal. (This will be for the three smaller vines.)
• Cut 12 berries from your red fabric.
• Cut 5 leaves from three different greens.
Directions for assembling these are on page 43 under Vines and Berries.
Follow the photo for placement.
• Appliqué your pattern pieces in place following the picture.
Trim the center block to 20 3/4" x 24 1/2".
• For the 3" wide border, cut your pieces 3 1/4" x widths of 2 1/2" to 4 1/2".
The number of pieces will depend on how you cut them. I have 37. Each corner piece will be cut 3 1/4" x 3 1/4". Have fun with it, there doesn't have to be a set size, just colors you like.

Gourds template on pp.10, 11and 33
Letters template on p. 17

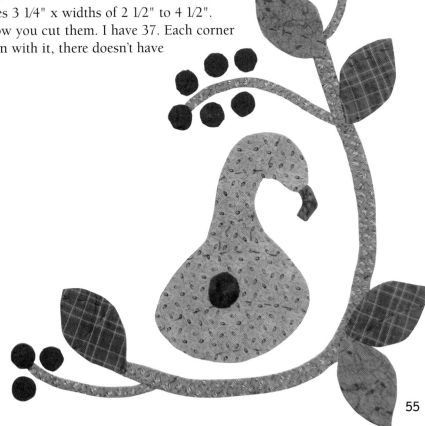

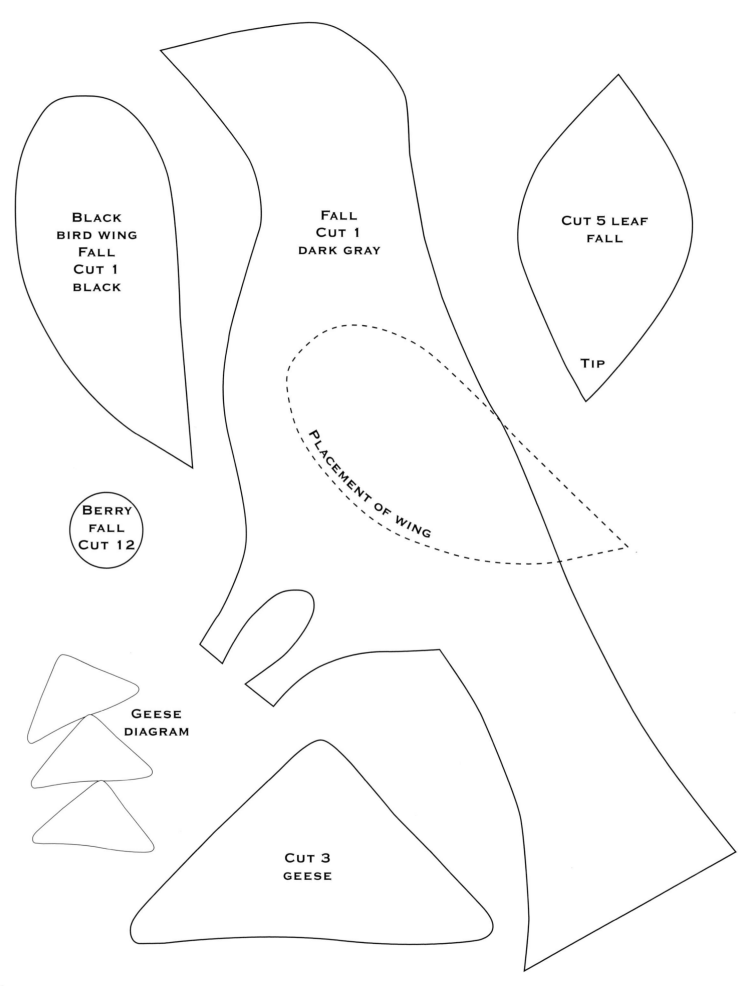

BLACK
bird wing
FALL
Cut 1
black

FALL
Cut 1
DARK GRAY

Cut 5 leaf
fall

Tip

PLACEMENT OF WING

BERRY
fall
Cut 12

GEESE
diagram

Cut 3
geese

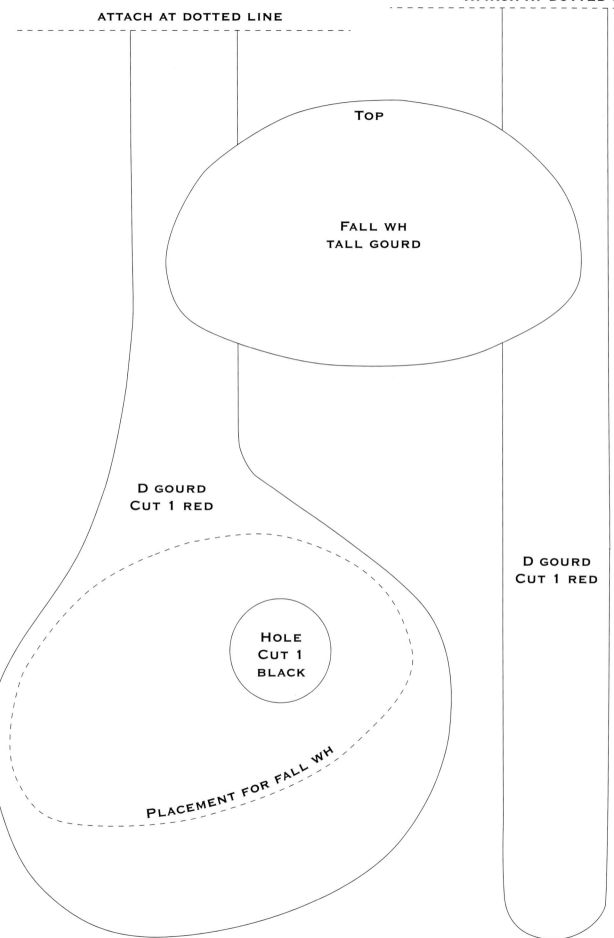

Add seam allowance on all appliqué pieces when cutting.

Finished size 27" x 29 1/4".

Fabric Requirements
- 3/8 yard blue and cream stripe for background
- A fat 8th of 5 different colors of prints and stripes for 5 rail fence block
- 11 different color 5" squares (charm packs work great for this kind of border)
- Scrap of red and cream stripe for cabin
- Scrap of black for windows
- Scraps of mottled creamy white for snowman
- Scraps of black check for hat
- Black seed beads for eyes and mouth
- Black 6-ply floss for arms
- Gray and white print for letters
- Scrap of blue for moon
- Scrap of gold for star
- Scraps of four different greens for tree
- Scraps of brown for trunk
- 3/4 yard for backing

Block Construction
(Finished center 18" x 20 3/4".)
- Background- Cut 4 rectangles 10" x 11 3/8". Cut two vertically and two horizontally on the stripe. Join a horizontal top left to a vertical top right and a vertical bottom left to a horizontal bottom right. Then join the top to the bottom. See photo.
- Line house up with bottom and baste in place, with snowman on left and tree on right.
Appliqué left side of house, roof, windows and then chimney (catch right side windows under chimney). Add moon, star and letters. Trim center to 18 1/2" x 21 1/4".
You will need 11 rail fence blocks for the border.
- Cut five complementary fabric strips 1 3/8" x 53" (this is total length needed for 11- 41/2" blocks—you can break this up into smaller lengths if needed). Sew the strips together lengthwise. Press one way. Your width will be 4 7/8" x 53" (or equivalent)
- Cut them into 11 - 4 1/2" blocks. Square up the end you started cutting from and toss the end piece.
- Rail fence blocks will now measure 4 7/8" x 4 1/2".

For the one-piece blocks, cut them as follows. (Diagram on p. 61)
- Cut right side corner pieces A and D: 4 1/2" x 4 7/8".
- Cut right side pieces B and C: 4 7/8" square.
- Cut left side pieces E, F, and G: 4 3/4" x 4 7/8".
- Cut top and bottom pieces H, I, J, and K: 4 1/2" x 5 1/8".
- Place all rail fence blocks perpendicular in the border.
- Remember to keep your block measurements going the right way for size, and stitch together as follows:
- Add RF to B to RF to C to RF and stitch to the right side of the center.
- Add G to RF to F to RF to E and stitch to the left side of the center.
Before attaching last block, match up to top to be sure corner blocks line up.
- Add RF to H to RF to I to RF to A. Add to top of wall hanging.
Before attaching last block, match up to top to be sure corner blocks line up.
- Add RF to J to RF to K to RF to D to the bottom (See diagram.)

To Finish
- Add the cotton batting and backing. Big-stitch and bind. Date and sign your work.

House template on pp. 26 and 27
Tree template on p. 32

TOP

WINTER
CUT 1
YELLOW

CUT 1
CHECK

CUT 1
ORANGE

CUT 3
BLACK

WINTER
CUT 1
BLUE

CUT 1
WHITE

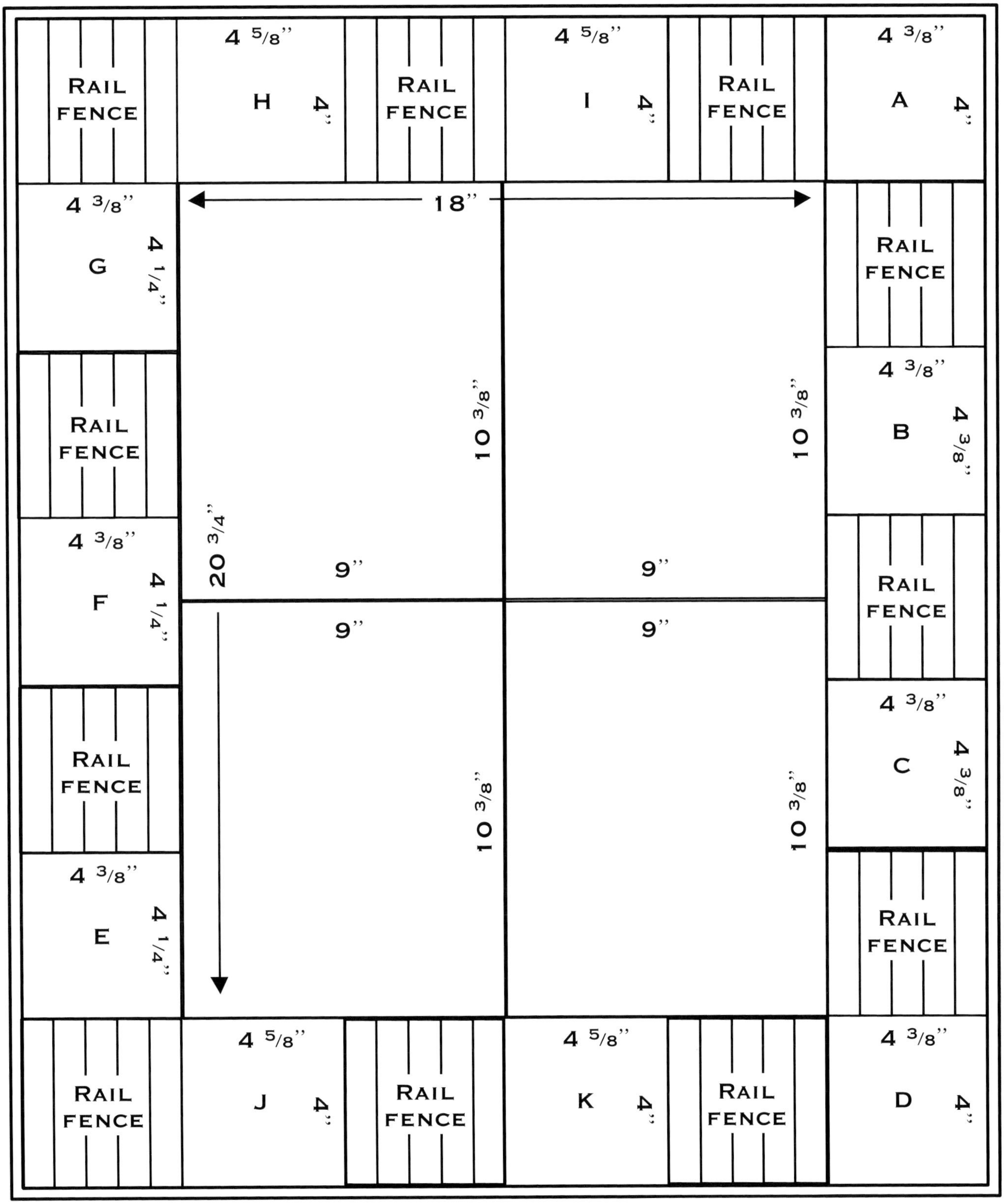

RAIL FENCE

4 5/8"   H   4"

RAIL FENCE

4 5/8"   I   4"

RAIL FENCE

4 3/8"   A   4"

4 3/8"   G   4 1/4"

◄———————— 18" ————————►

RAIL FENCE

RAIL FENCE

4 3/8"   B   4 3/8"

10 3/8"

10 3/8"

20 3/4"

9"

9"

4 3/8"   F   4 1/4"

9"

9"

RAIL FENCE

RAIL FENCE

4 3/8"   C   4 3/8"

10 3/8"

10 3/8"

4 3/8"   E   4 1/4"

RAIL FENCE

RAIL FENCE

4 5/8"   J   4"

RAIL FENCE

4 5/8"   K   4"

RAIL FENCE

4 3/8"   D   4"

Finished block sizes for Winter Wall Hanging
Place all rail fence blocks perpendicular.